Angels In My Heart

A Journey of Love and Loss

Kathleen Olowin

The original edition of this book was published in 2010 by Father's Press, LLC.

First Four Angels Press edition, 2020

ISBN: 978-1-7352628-0-2

For Zachary, Joshua, Victoria and Nicholas
forever in my heart

Angels In My Heart

A Journey of Love and Loss

Acknowledgments

Throughout the journey chronicled in this book, we have had the support of friends far too numerous to mention individually here. To all of you who supported us with prayers, hugs, emails and phone calls, we would not have survived all of this without you. You gave us the strength to go forward each day, and we can never express how grateful we are to all of you.

There are, however, specific thanks that need to be mentioned:

To my parents, Jack and Ellen Crowley, my brother Michael and my in-laws, Mary and Ron Olowin, for convincing me that I should listen to this crazy idea to write a book and for their unending support of the process.

To my dear friends Ron Conescu and Peggy Reed for giving me the thoughtful feedback that made my manuscript fuller and stronger.

To Judy and Michael Tashji for their beautiful work in designing the cover.

Most especially to Aaron without whose support and gifts of time, I could never have completed this project before the arrival of grandchildren.

Mary Jo and Aiden Burke, Sharon and Ken Forziati, Melissa and Carlos Vigil and Peggy Reed: You have shared each step of this journey—you have prayed with us and for us, brought us food, watched our children, and held our hands in sorrow and in joy. Truer friends we could never have.

Donna Vinal, Paul Klas and Kurt Elward: You have given this family not only the best medical care possible, but your prayers, love and support through fifteen very challenging years. You helped me to have the courage to keep going in this journey—we would not be raising these beautiful boys were it not for that support.

Matthew, Ryan, Tristan and Griffin: You are the miracles in my life, the incredible gifts from God for whom I am grateful every day.

Mom and Dad: You taught me through word and example what it means to have faith. I am blessed to have the love and support of such wonderful parents.

Aaron: You keep me grounded while lifting me up. Without you, this journey, these children, this life, simply would not be. You have always been and always will be the greatest gift in my life.

A note to my readers

If anyone had told me when I graduated college that one day I would be writing a book about miscarriage, I would have thought they were crazy. Although I took a minor concentration in English as an undergraduate, I had no aspirations to be a writer. At the time I got married, I had heard of miscarriage, but assumed it was something rare that would never happen to me. Little did I know how common it is, or how much I would come to know about it.

Each year, in the United States alone, nearly one million women experience the heartbreak of a miscarriage. An additional 26,000 families are faced with the trauma of a stillborn baby. The numbers are staggering, and yet, unless they know someone who has experienced this kind of a loss, most of these families feel very alone in their grief.

Every person's story is different, yet we all share common feelings and experiences as we try to come to terms with the death of our child. I don't profess to know all the answers—there is no magic formula which will suddenly make your world right again. The words I offer come merely from my own experience. But I hope, by sharing my journey with you, I can help with one small step of your healing.

You are not alone.

"Let the storms around you cease now
Let the storm within you end.
Let your mind and heart learn peace now.
As the calm that God will send.
God who brought you through the tempest
Guide your spirit home to mend."

—Marty Haugen
"The Song of Mark"

My Journey Of Love And Loss

1

I knew, a second before the impact, that we were going to get hit. The screech of brakes preceded the shock as the car crashed into us from behind, propelling our car forward several yards. As my head slammed back against the head rest, my first thought was "Oh, my God, the baby!" The panic that flooded me was quickly overtaken by the rational side of my brain, which told me, "You didn't hit the steering wheel; the baby is fine."

Since we had only one car, my husband, Aaron, usually walked to work, but sometimes I would take him if the weather was bad or he was running late. October 3, 1995 was a beautiful day, but Aaron had overslept. He was supposed to be at work at 7:30am, and since it was only a 10-minute round trip, I had just pulled on sweats and a T-shirt, planning to shower and eat once I got back.

After making sure I was okay, Aaron got out to check on the other driver, and I moved across to sit in the passenger's seat, since opening my door would have put me into oncoming traffic. I didn't dare stand up, as shaky as my legs were feeling, but sat there with my hand to my head, trying to calm my pounding heart. Aaron came back and reported that the other driver's airbag had deployed and he appeared unhurt. Aaron crouched by my open door and held my hand. Someone called 911.

After a few minutes, the rescue squad arrived. Sitting with my legs out the door and my feet on the ground, they began asking me questions. Are you feeling dizzy? Can you tell me what day it is? I knew they were trying to ascertain if I had hit my head. I assured them I had not hit the windshield but that my head had snapped forward and back into the head rest. One of the rescue workers had climbed into the car on the driver's side and was holding my head steady from behind, in case of a neck injury. After a few more questions, one of them glanced down to my baggy tee shirt.

"Ma'am, are you pregnant?"

"Yes, 32 weeks."

Suddenly, the topic of questions changed to concern over the baby. Are you having any pain? Is there any fluid leaking? No, nothing like that. They asked if I wanted to be taken to the hospital. Yes, I definitely wanted my midwife to check me out, just to be sure. Was our car drivable? I was shaky enough that I still had not stepped out to take a look at it. The response was a shake of the head.

"Then I guess you all need to take me."

With that statement, I was labeled a possible neck trauma, and a large collar was placed around my neck. The emergency technicians eased me onto a stretcher and strapped me down, loading me into the ambulance just like on TV. I'm sure the guy who hit us was panicking when he saw that. There were probably visions of law suits from the family of a pregnant woman flashing before his eyes. It looked like I was seriously hurt, but it was all just precautionary. I felt incredibly foolish. We don't need to make all this fuss, do we? Can't I just ride on the bench back here? Aaron got our things out of the car and rode in the front with the driver. On the way to the hospital, the technicians monitored the baby's heart rate, which remained good and strong.

When we got to Martha Jefferson Hospital, Aaron filled

2

out paperwork while I was taken back to an exam room so that the baby's heartbeat could be checked again. Once they had monitored the heartbeat for several minutes and had seen no signs of bleeding, fluid leaking, or contractions, everyone's worries over the baby seemed to relax. This little person seemed unconcerned about the traumas of the morning. They raised the head of the bed to a slant, but the collar remained in place. Aaron was brought back to wait with me. When the nurse found out he had also been in the car, she decided they should check him out as well, so he was put in the bed next to me with a collar on his neck. We went through X-rays and other tests that determined we both had a case of whiplash, but nothing more serious.

The ER staff had called my midwife's office and were told that she was upstairs on the Labor and Delivery floor with a patient. They paged her there and told her one of her patients had been brought into the ER from a car accident. Donna promised to be down when she was done.

By the time we were finished with all the tests it was almost 10 o'clock, and I had still not had anything to eat or drink. I hadn't even brushed my teeth before I left—this was definitely not how I had planned on spending my morning. The ER was fairly quiet, and while we were waiting for Donna, I finally asked one of the nurses if there was anything I could have to eat, since I had not had breakfast. She managed to find some cranberry juice and saltine crackers, which wasn't much of a breakfast, but after all the trauma of the morning, my stomach probably couldn't have handled much more, even if it had been offered.

When Donna finally appeared, she got the report on the baby's heartbeat monitoring from the nurse and then asked us what had happened. As we described the accident, she shook her head and commented that it must have been a bad morning out there because she had passed an accident on her way to the hospital that morning. She had contemplated stopping, as the rescue squad was not yet on the scene, but didn't want to leave her patient waiting, so she had gone on ahead.

"It was a bad one, though. The guy's airbag had gone off and everything."

"Where were you?" I asked.

"On Hydraulic, on my way to the bypass."

I gave her a little half wave. All the blood drained from her face.

"Oh, my God, you were in that car?"

"I was *driving* that car."

Donna stared at me, then glanced at Aaron, as if in doubt that we were both okay. I assured her the doctors had said we had no serious injuries. Then she got off the stool to examine me. As she did so, she commented it was probably a good thing she had decided not to stop. What would she have done if she had stopped to offer aid and been faced with one of her patients in the car? To leave her laboring patient waiting at the office would not have been fair, but she could not have left an expectant patient at the scene of an accident either. After checking me over, she monitored the baby's heart rate again. It was still steady and strong, and there were no signs of contractions. It had been almost three hours since the accident, and she decided that if I hadn't gone into labor by that point, I wasn't going to do so. I was released with a soft collar for my neck and orders to rest for the next several days.

A day or two later, the insurance company declared our car to be totaled, and we went to the junkyard to collect our personal things from the car. When the man behind the counter realized which car was ours he looked at my protruding belly and said to me,

"You weren't in that car, were you?"

"I was driving that car."

"You okay?"

I nodded. He shook his head and pointed us to the spot where our car was parked.

We had been at a full stop in a 1979 Ford Fairmont and

had been hit from behind at about 35 mph. For the first time, I understood the amazement people expressed at the fact that we had all walked away from the accident unhurt. The back right corner of the car was raised, buckled, and twisted, crushed into the back seat. The police officer who had brought us the accident report the day after the accident had told me that they had measured skid marks on the road for about forty feet leading up to the impact site. The driver had done everything in his power to stop the car—how much worse would it all have been if he hadn't slowed his car as much as he did? This baby must have a very special guardian angel, I thought.

Donna had made an appointment for me to come in a few days after the accident, just for a follow-up check on the baby. Aside from being sore, all was still well. We discussed the accident and how lucky we all were.

"God had angels watching over us," I told her.

"He had an angel between you and that steering wheel."

In the days that followed, the more I replayed the accident in my head, the more I came to agree with her. My head had snapped forward and back, but from the shoulders down I had not moved. Both the baby and I had come through an accident in a car with 16-year-old seat belts and no airbags, and all we had was some whiplash and a few bruises from the seat belt. Yes, I thought, there were angels there for sure.

I had been wearing my neck collar at home, but not when I was out. I didn't like the fuss people made when they saw it, and wearing it for long periods of time would irritate me. Donna had warned me that it would take me longer to heal from this accident than it would Aaron, since my body was also doing so much work preparing to birth a baby. My neck tired easily when I wasn't wearing the collar, but I had no other complaints aside from the normal aches and fatigue shared by all pregnant women as delivery draws near.

A few days before my due date, I began having regular contractions, but they were neither particularly painful nor did they get stronger and closer together. After a full day of mild contractions and several phone conversations with Donna, she decided this was "prodromal" or "false" labor. The uterus was getting ready for labor, but these contractions were not actually going to lead to delivery that day. Eventually, it would turn into active labor, but that could be several days away, by which point I would be exhausted. She told me to drink two glasses of wine and get some sleep. Wine? While I'm pregnant? She assured me that at this point it would do no harm, but would relax the uterus and put me and the baby to sleep. For someone who drinks a half a glass of wine on occasion, two glasses was a rather bitter prescription, one I had a hard time consuming. But it did the trick, and the contractions stopped.

In the early morning hours of December 6, 1995, one day before my due date, the real contractions began. I had decided early on in the pregnancy that I wanted to do this as naturally as possible, without an epidural or other medication. The idea of a needle in my spinal column gave me the shivers, and I had heard that oral or intravenous pain medication could have effects on a newborn. Donna was a proponent of natural child birth and had assured me there were lots of ways to try and manage the pain of labor without drugs. But she had also told me that I needed to listen to her if she said an epidural or other medication was necessary, for it would be because she knew I was tired and we still had a long way to go before delivery. Okay, I agreed, that's fair.

Aaron and I stayed at home through the night. When we arrived at Donna's office around 8:30 in the morning, I was only four centimeters dilated. As we got further into the labor and the contractions got harder, I began to have sharp pains in my back with each contraction. I had been prepared for labor pains in the abdomen, but not in the back. After trying massage and counter pressure for a while, Donna suggested I spend some time in the jacuzzi tub to see if that would help. Although it did provide some relief, I quickly came to a point where I was unable to breathe through the contractions as we had been taught in our childbirth class. The pain, combined with my asthmatic panic reaction that kicks in when I am having trouble breathing, caused me to begin to hyperventilate. Donna had me breathe into a brown paper bag between contractions to try to keep my oxygen supply level, but still my fingers and face felt tingly, like a limb that has gone to sleep. When I finally reached the point where I was being completely overwhelmed by the pain, it was too late to give me anything to help with it—Donna knew we were too close to delivery. She told me, "All I can do now is shoot you."

"Don't tempt me." I replied between breaths in the bag.

She was waiting for me to tell her that I needed to push, but that urge never came. Finally, she got me out of the tub to check and see what was happening and discovered that the baby's head was very close to delivery. The nurses quickly got me up into the bed. The moment I began to push the pain seemed to disappear. I was in control now. I felt strong inside. I could do this.

After thirty minutes of focused pushing, the baby's head emerged and Donna told me not to push while she suctioned the nose and mouth. She then offered Aaron the opportunity to "catch" the baby, which he declined with a wide-eyed shake of the head. On one final push, Matthew Ian entered the world, a beautiful 7 lbs 15-½ oz. Donna lifted him straight to my stomach, where he lay quietly blinking at me. I ran my finger gently down the side of his head and gazed at this perfect little miracle while Aaron cut the umbilical cord. All the years of longing and waiting to be a mother were over.

Other than being dehydrated from so much time in the jacuzzi tub, I recovered very quickly. A few weeks later, I passed what looked like a cashew nut, small and gray, about the size of the first joint on my thumb. Was this what it appeared to be, an embryo? I searched through my pregnancy materials until I found the magazine with pictures of an embryo at various stages of development. What I had just passed looked remarkably like a six week old embryo.

I thought back to my first prenatal appointment with Donna, at nine weeks. Though it was early, she had listened to see if she could hear the heartbeat—and to everyone's surprise, she did. As she listened, she said,

"Hmm, do I hear two?"

"Oh, don't joke about that!" we laughed nervously. I figured she probably said that to all her newly expectant moms, just to see their reactions. No, she was serious. As much as I longed to be a mother, twins had never crossed my mind. Donna listened for a bit and could not decide what she was hearing, but she did not see a reason to order an ultrasound either. It was still early enough in the pregnancy that the heartbeat was fairly soft and hard to hear clearly. On our next visit, there was one strong heartbeat, and Donna decided it must have been just an echo she had heard previously.

After looking at the magazine picture, I called Donna, and described what I had just seen. She said that it was too early after delivery for me to have conceived and miscarried and that the labor and delivery staff make sure no tissue is left behind after delivery. There was no reason for me to come in to see her until my postpartum checkup, still a few weeks away. I hung up with the vague feeling that there was something she wasn't telling me.

Although I did not mention it to anyone except Aaron, my thoughts kept coming back to the experience over the next few days. Was that really an embryo? Had there been two babies at one point? With no way to answer that question, I finally put it out of my mind. After all, I had a beautiful, healthy son.

2

As Matthew approached his second birthday, we were beginning to think about having a second child. But I had been having a great deal of trouble with my asthma in recent months, and we were advised to wait on a pregnancy until my body had had time to recover and get strong again.

In the spring of 1998, Dr. Klas and I tried a new combination of medications to help me through the pollen season. At the end of May, when I had survived the allergy season without too much difficulty, both Donna and Dr. Klas felt I was strong enough and gave us the green light to think about another baby after I weaned back to my basic daily medication. Since we had had no trouble conceiving Matthew and had had an uneventful pregnancy, it didn't occur to me that the next time would be any different.

In early August, I was feeling some early pregnancy symptoms. The time for my menstrual cycle came and went, but I waited a few more days before taking a home pregnancy test. Maybe, I thought, it is just wishful thinking. My cycles had never been a regular 28 days. By day 35, I felt it was time to check. When the test came back negative, I thought, well, not this month. But as each day of the next week went by with no cycle, I began to get more hopeful. At the end of the week I took another test, expecting to see a positive result. It was still negative.

I felt disheartened, but even more I was confused—even

for my irregular cycles, this was long. It had been six weeks since my last one. Besides, I wasn't feeling quite right. My stomach felt funny and I was feeling very draggy, like I hadn't gotten enough sleep for nights in a row. I had been very tired in the first trimester of Matthew's pregnancy and had napped a great deal in the afternoons. People often say you can be much more tired during your second pregnancy, since you are also caring for the first child, but this seemed much too early to be feeling the level of exhaustion I was experiencing. I wasn't even registering a positive test. And yet, by this point, the test should have registered positive if I was pregnant. My body was telling me one thing, the urine test something else. How could I be experiencing the symptoms of pregnancy and not be pregnant?

A few days later, I started spotting. I was bleeding, but very lightly and inconsistently. It was not like my regular cycle, so I called Donna and described the last few weeks. She said most likely it was a "subcutaneous miscarriage." I had conceived, but the egg had not implanted. It was just taking my body a while to figure it out. She said these situations are very common—most of the time, the woman doesn't even know anything happened. But when you are trying to conceive, you are aware of every little symptom, all month long. The regular cycle should start up soon, she counseled me, but she warned me not to be surprised if it was unusually heavy. The hormones in my body had been preparing my uterus to carry a pregnancy, so the uterine lining would be thicker, and there would be more to shed than in normal months. Unless I felt there was something wrong, she didn't need to see me. She told me to call her in a week.

What do I tell Aaron, I wondered, as I hung up the phone. I hadn't told him about any of this yet, since there wasn't really anything to tell—the tests had come back negative. But I was having a miscarriage. Or was I? If I was never really pregnant, could it really be considered a miscarriage? Either way, Aaron needed to know what was happening. That night

I told him I had hoped to have happy news to share with him, and then relayed the conversation with Donna. He did not know quite what to say. He seemed to find his role in offering comfort to me. But I didn't know what to think of this myself. The bleeding did start up, and though it never got particularly heavy, it did continue for a bit longer than usual. When I phoned Donna at the end of the week, she figured it had taken care of itself. The next month's cycle could be thrown off a bit, she counseled, and told me not to be concerned if it went longer than usual before the next month's cycle began.

A week after the cycle ended, the bleeding began again. My cycles sometimes stopped and started again, but never with such a long break. I called Donna. Sometimes this happens with a miscarriage, she said. It is taking your body longer to clean out than we thought. Just like after delivering a baby, the bleeding can continue for several weeks.

Oh, great.

For most of my adolescence, I had had to deal with painful menstrual cramps each month. Most of those months would require Advil and a heating pad to relieve the pains that would have me curling up into a ball. But now, in the midst of a miscarriage, I did not have menstrual cramps at all. The bleeding was light and there was no pain involved. It just didn't seem to ever stop. Rather like trying to empty a container of water a few drops at a time, the bleeding continued to stop and start, stop and start, never getting very heavy, but never resolving either.

I began to feel very worn out. I would have a day with no bleeding and just when I would begin to hope that it was finally over, it would begin again. Each time that happened I got a little more depressed. Isn't this ever going to end? It was beginning to drain me physically and emotionally. Every time the bleeding began again, it weighed down my spirit. And the exhaustion continued—a tired that went deep into my bones. It was far worse than it had been during my pregnancy with

Matthew. I have never before felt fatigue like that, not even during the sleep-deprived months of having a newborn child. I would lie down when Matthew took a nap and fall instantly into a deep, deep sleep, only to wake up two hours later feeling just as tired. Donna said later that my body was trying very hard to hold on to that pregnancy. It didn't want to let go.

I hadn't really told anyone else what was happening. I wasn't keeping it a secret, but it was hard to share with people because I wasn't sure how to explain what was happening. My parents were out of the country on vacation, and this was not an emergency that warranted a transatlantic phone call. The few friends that I did tell, I told over email, just after my initial conversation with Donna. I explained what she had said, but told them it wasn't really a miscarriage, since the baby had never really started to develop. It would be easier on my mind and body having this happen so early, I rationalized. I wasn't attached to anything yet, right? After all, since the tests had come back negative, I wasn't really losing a pregnancy. I was losing the idea of possibly being pregnant. It shouldn't be too hard to get passed that and begin looking ahead again. Right?

One of my friends from my women's prayer group, Terri, wrote back and told me it didn't matter if I had ever been "officially" pregnant, conception had occurred and this miscarriage was real, just very early. The more I heard the term miscarriage in reference to what was happening, the more I began to think in terms of having lost a baby. Terri had told me that a loss is a loss, no matter when it happens. It is okay to grieve. But emotionally I was numb, fatigued with constantly waiting to see if the bleeding would begin again. How can you move past something emotionally for which there is a daily physical reminder?

As the weeks of off-again/on-again bleeding continued, my emotional state began to be affected more and more. I was edgy, frustrated and weary. And though Aaron was very supportive and sweet, bringing me flowers and letting me rest as I needed, he really didn't seem affected by any of this. It was something that was happening to me. I could talk to him about the growing sadness I felt at the loss of this child, but he did not share in that sadness. He didn't seem to be thinking about the fact that this would have been his baby as well. It seemed like he was treating this more as an illness from which I was trying to recover—he did what he would have done to help if I had had the flu, taking over some of the housework and playing with Matthew while I napped. As the weeks went by, I felt increasingly in my own little world, with Aaron on the outside looking in.

By the second week in September, I had been bleeding for almost five weeks. I called Donna again. I was unprepared to hear her to say that we needed to do a dilation and curtage, or D&C. I was so tired of the whole thing, and I agreed with her that it had been going on much too long, but surgery? I hadn't even considered that possibility. However, she was beginning to be concerned that I might become anemic from the prolonged bleeding. And the risk of an infection developing increased the longer this went on. It was time to put an end to it.

As a midwife, Donna is not licensed to perform surgery, so she transferred my care temporarily to Dr. Wolanski, the OB-GYN with whom she shared the practice. Wednesdays are his surgery days, so she put me on his schedule for the following Wednesday. Knowing I had to go through surgery was bad enough—now I had to wait for it also. Everything in my day to day life was now entwined with what was happening in my body. I wished we could just get it over and be done with it.

That weekend I found an ad in the Sunday paper for a silver cross that had footprints across the front. On the back was the last verse of my favorite poem, "Footprints": "It was then that I carried you." This poem speaks of walking the beach in the company of God, and it had been a favorite of mine since I had first read it sometime in high school. Walking on the beach has always been one the things I love best about going to the ocean. I particularly like the early morning to walk, the most peaceful time at the shore, for I feel the presence of God in the quiet voice of the ocean. I had recently lost the small silver cross I had worn daily for years, and I missed having it around my neck. Although I don't usually spend money on jewelry, I really liked this cross and decided I was going to buy it for myself. It was too big to be the one I wore all the time, but I needed something to help me feel happier right now, and the reminder that God is always there would be a comfort. Of course, these ads say "allow 2-3 weeks for delivery," so I suspected it would be quite a while before I received it.

I went to the hospital on Monday and had blood drawn for the pre-operative work-up. The two days of waiting until the surgery seemed to drag on endlessly. My body was already tired, and the pending procedure weighed on me, making my body feel heavy and slow. And the knowledge of why it was needed weighed on my spirit. I tried not to think about it, yet it was always in my consciousness, like a cloud hovering just over my shoulder.

The surgery was not until Wednesday afternoon, so Aaron went to work in the morning, and I picked him up on the way to get Matthew from preschool. Terri had agreed to watch Matthew for us that afternoon—her son, David, was just a few weeks younger than Matthew, and we often got together to let the boys play.

It was an outpatient procedure, so we headed up to the day surgery wing. While we were waiting in my small room, Dr. Wolanski came in to talk to us and explain what would happen. He would forcibly open the cervix enough to be able to clean out the lining of the uterus. Sometimes this is done with scraping tools and sometimes through vacuum extraction. The decision would be made based upon what he found once he was able to view the inside of the uterus. He offered me the choice of being awake and just having a spinal block or being put under general anesthesia; he cautioned that most women prefer not to be awake. No, I definitely don't need to remember this, thank you, I thought. Put me out.

He also gave us the reports of the blood work that had been done on Monday. The pregnancy hormones were low, but they were elevated enough to tell him that indeed conception had occurred. That, at least, validated the need for the D&C and removed all doubt as to whether I had actually been pregnant.

In the beginning of this ordeal, it had been difficult to think in terms of losing a baby. Because I did not have a positive pregnancy test, in my head it hadn't been a real pregnancy. But as a Catholic, I believe that life begins at conception. Dr. Wolanski had just confirmed through the blood work that conception had occurred. For the first time, I truly believed I had lost a baby. She or he was tiny, had lived only for a few days, but had lived nonetheless. My baby had died.

When they took me into the operating room, I lay staring up at the bright lights over the operating table. There was very little talk in the room as the staff made the final preparations for the procedure. There were few risks to the surgery, so the nurses did not need to reassure me that everything would be fine. And what could they say to make me feel any better about why I was there?

While I was in recovery, Dr. Wolanski stopped in our room to tell Aaron that everything had gone fine. Once I was back in the room, he came back and told us that there had been "some tissue" caught that was preventing things from resolving naturally. He had cleaned out the uterus and found nothing unusual. There were no fibroid tumors or physical defects to the uterus that would be cause for concern.

After an hour or so in my room, when the liquids they had given me to drink were staying down, Dr. Wolanski discharged me with instructions to take it easy for the next day or two. I should recover fairly quickly.

When we got home from the hospital after picking up Matthew, I went to retrieve the mail. There was a small package with my name on it. Inside was the cross I had ordered. I had only mailed the order on Monday—even if the order arrived on Tuesday and the package had been mailed the same day, delivery was awfully fast. Someone knew I needed this cross right now.

3

The anesthesia had left me feeling tired and foggy, and I went straight to my bed once we got inside. I slept off and on for the rest of the day while Aaron took care of Matthew.

It took me several days to recover from the surgery, longer than I expected. My insides felt battered and bruised, and I was still so very tired. Terri reminded me that it was not just the surgery from which I needed to recover. It was everything my body had been dealing with for the past two months.

Aaron had been trying very hard to be supportive, but he had no way to really understand what I was feeling. I didn't even know what I was feeling, other than empty. But he didn't seem to be feeling anything at all. He seemed so far away from me. I felt like there was a large gulf between us that had been growing throughout this ordeal, and it was one we couldn't bridge. On one side, he was going about his life as usual and I was lost and alone on the other. Going through the surgery experience with me had made it a bit more real to him, but he still was not looking at it as the loss of a child. To him, it seemed a "missed opportunity."

A week after my surgery, we went to Camp Trinity, an annual family retreat weekend given by my parents' church. Saturday morning I got up and went to the morning prayer service while Matthew and Aaron were still asleep. The sun was just coming up, and the mist was rising off of the pond across from the second-floor porch as we gathered in the chilly air. The musicians had set themselves up at the outermost end of the porch, and the group of about thirty people had made a large circle along the railings and the back wall of the building.

Halfway through the service, the woman leading the singing invited anyone who wished to come forward and take a flower from the bucket by the table and place it in the vase in memory of someone they had lost. Tears began to silently slide down my cheeks. I had been to the Saturday morning service many times over the years, but I had forgotten this annual ritual. Perhaps if I had remembered it, I would not have gone. My parents were not there that morning, Aaron and Matthew were not there, and no one at Camp Trinity knew what I had just experienced. I felt alone in the crowd.

As I stood with my back resting against the supports of the second-floor railing with tears running down my face, I sensed the presence of arms come around me from behind, and I felt a voice whisper to me, "You are not alone. You can do this. Go ahead." I took a deep breath and gathered my courage to make the short walk to the table in the middle of the circle. I put the flower in the vase for "someone special" and returned to my spot by the railing.

A few minutes later, the service ended with the exchange of greetings of peace, and I found myself greeting a long-time family friend, Chris. "Are you okay?" she asked.

"No, not really." I knew she had seen my tears.

She touched my shoulder. "Who did you put the flower in for?"

The tears welled up again as I told her I had just had a miscarriage.

She enfolded me in a big hug. "I've been there, twice. I understand." The hug was more than just a friendly greeting. It had a depth to it that made me feel that perhaps someone did understand.

She warned me: "Make sure you are not alone on your due date."

Due date? I had never even gotten to the point of going to my first prenatal visit. "I don't have a due date," I told her, looking her in the eye for the first time.

She smiled and rubbed my shoulder. "But you know when this baby would have been due."

I nodded, slowly. "Sometime in the third week of April." Even without a prenatal visit, I could calculate the months.

Chris smiled softly and squeezed my arm. "Don't be alone."

Later in the weekend, I thanked Chris again for her support. I was so glad she had been there that morning. I told her about the experience at the railing of feeling hugged from behind when no one was there. I felt the presence of an angel there, and I am pretty sure that angel told me, "Now, go find Chris" as the service ended. God knew that I needed someone to provide a bit of comfort right then, and no one can do that better than someone who has been through it herself.

4

The process of working through the grief really began after Camp Trinity. I had not been able to deal with the emotional aspects of this loss until the physical sensations went away. But once we had taken care of that, the emotions hit hard. Terri knew right away when she saw me a few days after that retreat.

"How are you? It hit, didn't it?" The sadness must have shown on my face.

"Is it that obvious?" I asked.

"No, only if you know what to look for. I've been waiting for it. It had to come out at some point."

Terri had lost a baby at 20 weeks, before we had become friends. In talking with her, at first I wondered what right do I have to be upset over my loss? Look at what Terri had gone through—this was nowhere near the same thing! But Terri continued to tell me that it doesn't matter if you are pregnant for several months or only a day—you lost a baby, and it's okay to grieve. Never once did she tell me her situation had been worse or more real for having happened later. Slowly, I began to see that if she was giving me permission to see our situations as equal, it was okay for to me to feel sad.

Several friends recommended books to me during this time, some on miscarriage, some just on grief. I had majored in psychology; I knew all about the stages of grief. The numbness of disbelief gives way to anger over the loss.

Irritability, anxiety, and guilt can all be a part of that stage. Then after a while, depression sets in and finally, over time, acceptance. But it's one thing to know about grief; it's another thing to grieve. I had felt sadness when my grandparents had died—but nothing like the feeling of loss I now experienced. Knowing what stages of grief to expect did not make them go any faster. And the one person I really wanted to share this with wasn't experiencing our situation the same way I was.

Anger is a part of any grief process, and it needs to come out in some way. For me, most of it was directed at Aaron, though I tried hard not to let it actually show. I was angry that he didn't share my sadness and loss. He was still viewing this as a missed opportunity. My head understood why he didn't feel the same way I did. Because, in this pregnancy, he had never been an expectant father, he felt no sense of loss. It is hard to miss something you never knew you had. And he had not endured any of the physical loss, the bleeding, the surgery. How could he possibly see all this the same way I did? And yet, it was his baby, too. Why didn't he feel sad that we would never get to raise this child? I knew it would not be fair to let the anger come out at him for something he was unable to control. It would only hurt him and make him angry in response. But that didn't change the fact that I felt I was getting more support from my friends than from my spouse.

One night when we were talking, Aaron commented that "something important happened to you..." At that, the anger did erupt. "NO!" I screamed. "To US! Something happened to US!"

But he had really summed it up. It had happened to me. I was dealing with this alone. What should have been our joy was my loss. And that just wasn't fair.

I began to view that early morning service at Camp Trinity as symbolic of the whole experience. I was there alone. Aaron and Matthew weren't there; my parents weren't there— none of the people closest to me were there to comfort me. And yet I was not alone, for the presence of God was very strong. The feeling of those arms around me let me know that even though I felt alone in the crowd, I was never actually alone. God was right there with me and would never leave.

While my head understood that, my heart felt so alone. Aaron seemed so far away and I desperately wanted to bridge the gap I felt between us. But I couldn't figure out how.

I had a long conversation about this dilemma with Sister Pat at our church. Sr. Pat suggested to me that perhaps we would not be able to bridge it. Perhaps this was one of those times in life when I must stand alone with God.

I felt more peaceful after that. Accepting that maybe Aaron couldn't enter that circle made it easier not to direct my anger at him.

In the middle of October, about three weeks after the retreat, I saw Dr. Wolanski for my post-operative check-up. My cycle started again that morning; as he had predicted, my flow was very heavy. I called the office to ask if I should reschedule the appointment. Don't worry about it, I was told. He's used to doing exams this way.

He might be. I'm not.

Though the exam was not any more uncomfortable, physically, than a regular GYN check-up, having the waterproof pads put under me to absorb the blood flow while he poked and prodded made me feel even more exposed than usual.

"You're fine," he told me after the exam. "You're healed. Even your cycle seems back on track." Physically, he told me, my body was healthy. There was no reason to wait if Aaron and I wanted to get pregnant again.

What are the chances of having to go through all this again, I asked him. He shook his head.

"Your risks are no higher than anyone else's. One in four pregnancies ends in miscarriage. It doesn't mean anything about subsequent pregnancies."

Yet I felt crummy: strong cramps and fatigue, just like I'd had as an adolescent. And hearing "you're healed!" made the whole ordeal seem terribly final. This chapter was finished, but I wasn't done with the grieving. Physically and emotionally, I felt awful.

Donna pointed out that after a delivery—whether a full-term baby or a miscarriage—a woman's body goes on a hormonal roller-coaster ride for about six weeks. I felt awful, and that was normal. But when you have a healthy baby, she said, you have something positive to offset the negative effects of the hormones. With a miscarriage, there is no positive.

Matthew was definitely something positive. I had a little boy who needed me and who brought some joy into my life. Often, though, I did not feel I was doing a good job as a mother. It is hard to have patience when you don't feel well, and I had had several months of not feeling well either physically or emotionally. There were many days when I felt like a failure as a mother for snapping at him or losing my patience much too easily. Other people kept reassuring me that I was doing fine, and so was Matthew. Sr. Pat told me that these few months would be just a drop in the bucket of Matthew's life. He most likely would not remember them later, since he was not even three, and I was certainly not scarring him for life because I was easily frustrated. It was not until I realized that anyone not feeling well is not going to perform up to his or her potential that I began to cut myself a little slack.

After reading the suggestion in several books about miscarriage, I approached Aaron about choosing a name for our baby. Sr. Pat had told me that "this was a life, no matter how long or short. There is a soul in Heaven, and someday you will be reunited." Then shouldn't we know him or her by name?

Aaron agreed, and we began to mull over the possibilities. When I asked him a few days later if he had given it any thought, I was surprised to hear him say yes, but that he had only been coming up with boys' names. We decided we didn't want to pick a "neutral" name, as some books suggested, so we prayed about it, asking if there was any way for God to let us know if it had been a boy or a girl. Over a few days of asking, I felt a little voice keep whispering, "It was a boy." When I mentioned to Aaron that I had a feeling it had been a boy, and he answered, "Me, too." We spent time with our baby name book, looking at the meanings of names, and we chose the name Joshua Caelan. Joshua means "God is my salvation," and Caelan is the Scottish form of Nicholas, the patron saint of children.

In the Catholic church, the month of November is set aside to remember those who have died. Our church had the "Book of the Dead" on display all month, for those who wished to enter the names of anyone they had lost. A large, bound volume, with a fresh page for each year, it sat on a pedestal near the baptismal font just inside the entrance to the church. Shortly after choosing Joshua's name, we decided to enter it into the book. Our friend Brian was at mass that morning, and we asked him if he would be willing to be with us when we wrote the baby's name in the book. He told us he would be honored, and we waited around in the hall after mass until everyone was gone. I didn't want to inscribe Joshua's name with crowds of people talking as they passed on their way out of church.

The lights had been turned off, and the church was empty when we wrote "Joshua Caelan Olowin" at the top of the next page of the book. Having Brian there was wonderful for the support; even more important, having one other person witness that simple little act somehow validated Joshua's existence.

The process of selecting a name for Joshua had made the situation a little more real to Aaron. He was still not feeling the depth of emotion that I had been struggling with, but at least choosing a name forced him to think in terms of a person and not just an opportunity. He might never grieve this baby the way I was, but slowly the gap between us was beginning to close.

A week or so later, I was browsing in a Christmas shop in downtown Charlottesville when I came across an angel ornament, a little boy dressed in jeans and sneakers. He had a frog in the pocket of his robe and was blond just like Matthew. I suddenly thought that this is what Joshua might have looked like. When I purchased it, the woman at the counter offered to personalize it for me, so I had her write his name on the edge of the angel robe. Now we would have a special spot on our Christmas tree for our little angel in Heaven.

5

We had been told by Dr. Wolanski to wait one full cycle after the surgery but that there was no other need to wait before conceiving again. He assured us that this kind of thing happens frequently; just because we had had one miscarriage didn't mean we were likely to have a second one.

I was beginning to feel "ready" to have another baby, but I was also very scared. Miscarriage robs you not only of your baby, but also of the expectant joy of any subsequent pregnancies. I asked Terri how I was supposed to get over the fear. She said "You don't. You just live through it." No matter how hard you try, there will always be fear to overcome in getting pregnant again.

Since there was no way to "get over" the fear, I figured there was no more reason to wait in having another baby. As Thanksgiving passed by, I began to suspect that I might be pregnant. I had noticed the early signs, but I did not want to be too hopeful. I tried hard not to think about it, but that was pretty near impossible.

When we were almost a week past the time when my cycle should have begun, I decided it was time to find out. On the morning of December 6, 1998, Matthew's third birthday, I got up early to take a home pregnancy test. I was very apprehensive. What if it came back negative? Would we be starting all over again? I didn't want to stare at the stick during the two minutes of waiting and tried to busy myself with brushing my teeth, all the while nervously counting off seconds in my head. I replaced my toothbrush in the holder, took a deep breath and glanced at the stick. Two dark pink lines told me the test was positive.

I got back into bed and told Aaron I had good news for him. He hugged me tight and we marveled at the thought of starting all over again with a new baby. Matthew was very much a little boy now, running, talking, going to preschool. Part of me was a little overwhelmed at the idea of starting with a newborn again. But mostly, my heart was bursting with happiness. Please, Lord, I thought, let this baby grow healthy and strong. We should tell our families at Christmas, we decided. What a nice gift to give them!

I called Donna to tell her, and she told me she wanted me to go to the hospital to confirm the pregnancy with blood work and an ultrasound. Since we were just at five weeks, there was no way to confirm the pregnancy in the office—the heartbeat would not be audible for at least another month. But the sound waves used to create a picture of the inside of the uterus in an ultrasound should be able to give us an image of the tiny heartbeat. She scheduled the ultrasound for December 22nd. At that point, we would be just over seven weeks and should be able to see everything we needed to see. In the meanwhile, the blood work would at least make sure that the pregnancy hormone levels were increasing as they should.

I went in to Martha Jefferson twice that week, two days apart, and had the blood drawn. I remember thinking after the second draw that it had been less than a week since we found out I was pregnant. I was feeling similar to the way I had with Matthew's pregnancy, queasy and a little tired, but we were not yet past the point at which we had lost Joshua. This pregnancy had the potential to feel very long.

On December 11th, Donna called with the results of the blood work. The hormone levels seemed pretty good. Between the two blood draws, the levels had not quite doubled, but were within the comfort zone, so she was content. The news didn't surprise me. I hadn't been too worried over the blood work. It was, after all, just a confirmation that all was fine.

One week later, I was attending a meeting at church and stopped to use the bathroom on the way out. My heart about stopped when I saw blood on my underwear. Anxiety had me gripping the steering wheel as I fought the tears all the way home, praying "Please, Lord, please. Don't let me lose this baby, too." I called Donna as soon as I got home, and she said as long as it wasn't more than two tablespoons a day, everything should be fine. Lots of women spot during the first trimester. She told me to call if it got worse, and we would go ahead with the ultrasound as scheduled on the 22nd. Although she was calm and matter of fact, the call did little to ease my anxiety and fear.

When Matthew was having his quiet time in his room that afternoon, I lay down and tried to rest on the sofa. The bleeding had become more of a residual staining, but I began having a pain on my right side. When it hadn't gone away by late afternoon, I called Donna again. Since the pain and the bleeding were not getting worse, the chance of it being an ectopic pregnancy were slim, but she decided we should do the ultrasound the next day just to be sure. In an ectopic pregnancy, the egg implants in the wall of the fallopian tube instead of in the uterus. The mother experiences all the signs of a normal pregnancy until the embryo grows too big and ruptures the fallopian tube. This usually results in emergency surgery and removal of the tube, and can cause life threatening complications for the mother if left untreated. Donna assured me that it was an unlikely cause of the pain. She thought it was more likely an ovarian cyst, which are very common. If they rupture, they can cause pain for a few days, but otherwise are nothing to worry about. However, since I had not had any bleeding with Matthew's pregnancy, she understood that I was feeling frightened. She decided to have more blood drawn as well, so we could figure out what was happening.

The next day I dropped Matthew off at preschool and drove to Donna's office to pick up the paperwork I needed for the hospital. Because her office is small and does not have laboratory facilities or expensive ultrasound equipment, all prenatal tests must be done at the hospital. I walked across the street, registered at the hospital, and drove back to Matthew's school for the music program being performed for the parents. Having the music program to attend was a welcome distraction from the day, which felt very heavy. But it couldn't break the fear that gripped my heart. After the program, I returned to Martha Jefferson to have blood drawn. I felt I was existing in a fog, almost doing things on auto pilot. As I was driving around town, back and forth, I had a feeling that I had already lost this baby.

I kept telling myself not to worry and to just trust all was going to be okay. Deep breaths, I told myself. Let go of the anxiety, give it to God. But the tears kept threatening to escape—I blinked them back repeatedly as I drove around town. I tried to pray for the baby but found it too difficult. Finally, I just gave up and prayed for strength instead. The bleeding had begun again and, though it was still not more than just heavy spotting, it strengthened the fear being held in my heart.

I had called Terri the night before and told her what was going on. She tried to be reassuring, telling me that she had bled through half of David's pregnancy. She offered to take Matthew while Aaron went with me for the ultrasound. I couldn't imagine going in for this test by myself, but agreed it was probably better not have Matthew with us. We dropped Matthew off with Terri on our way to the hospital, and she gave me a reassuring hug. "Hold on to the positive things," she said. What would those be, I wondered. But I knew she was worried, too.

When an ultrasound is done later in a pregnancy, there is

29

amniotic fluid around the baby that provides a surface for the sound waves to bounce off. But at the early stage we were in, there was not yet fluid around the baby, and the uterus was still small enough to be far away from the surface of the abdomen. I needed to have a very full bladder for the technician to have something off of which to bounce the sound waves. I had been drinking the sixteen ounces of water I had been told to drink as I drove around town and was beginning to feel my bladder rather uncomfortably.

At the hospital, Aaron and I had to wait a long time for the ultrasound. There were magazines on the table in the waiting room, but neither of us tried to read. We tried to talk while we waited but found it just too difficult. What was there either of us could say to make the other feel better? It will be fine? We didn't know that. We ended up just sitting in silence, gripping each other by the hand. The strength of Aaron's hand in mine told me that already this experience would be different from what we went through with Joshua. Aaron was trying to give me strength, but I could tell he was just as scared as I was. No matter what the ultrasound showed, good news or bad, we were in this together.

Finally, the technician called us into the exam room. She placed a cold gel on my abdomen to make it easier to move the probe, and began the scan. It was very quiet. The monitor was turned away from me, but Aaron was able to see the screen from where he sat. The silence scrapped on my nerves, until finally I asked her if she was finding anything. She said no, but since it was still very early in the pregnancy, we might not be able to detect anything with the external exam. She would have to do the more detailed vaginal scan.

She wiped the gel off of my abdomen and told me I could use the bathroom before she proceeded with the internal scan. Because this time the probe would be inserted directly into the vagina, it would be closer to the uterus. There was no need to have a full bladder. The relief I felt in no longer having to endure a painfully full bladder did nothing to calm my growing anxiety.

The discomfort of having the probe inserted and moved around was enough to make me wish she would hurry and finish the scan. And yet, I was willing to endure it as long as it took if she could reassure us that everything was fine. However, she was unable to find anything conclusive with that scan either. There might have been the start of the amniotic sac forming, but it was not clear. She told us it was not a reason to panic—it was just too early to tell for sure. We'd repeat the exam in a week or two. We left the hospital subdued, but feeling there might still be hope.

We picked up Matthew, and Terri tried again to be reassuring. I wanted to believe there was still hope and tried to put on a positive front. The anxiety had diminished some with the technician words and I decided to try and hold on to the thoughts of it being just too early to see anything. I dropped Aaron back off at work and took Matthew home.

We had not been in the house for five minutes when Donna called. The story the technician had told her was much different from our earlier conversation. According to Donna, she should have been able to see something between the two tests. The hormone levels in the blood work had dropped since the last blood draw—they were even lower than the first day we had drawn. Donna said we could repeat the tests in a few days, for there are always fallibility factors in these things.

"But you are expecting the bleeding to pick up over the weekend, aren't you?" I asked.

"Most likely, yes."

I held it together fairly well while talking with her, but once I hung up the phone, I burst into tears. Poor Matthew did not know what to do when he found me sobbing in the kitchen, and he tried hard to make me feel better.

"Mama, what's wrong? Why you crying?"

"You want some cold water, Mama? How about more bagel?"

It must have been scary for him to see me so upset. I tried to pull myself together for his sake. I called Aaron at work, barely getting through the story without breaking down again: Donna had called, and it wasn't good news. Could he please come home? As we were still a one-car family, he asked if I could pick him up. No, I didn't trust myself to drive. Aaron said he would find a ride and be home within half an hour.

Why had the technician left us feeling there was still hope? If she knew there was nothing viable on the screen, why didn't she tell us that? Although I knew that her job was just to do the scans and give results to the doctors, not inform patients of problems, it made me angry that we had been allowed to think things were still okay. If nothing else, a doctor could have come into the room to give us the news. Aaron would have come home with me when we left the hospital instead of going back to work. This was news we should have received together. Why was it taking him so long to get home? The minutes ticked by so slowly.

I was sitting on Matthew's mattress trying to read to him when I heard Aaron come in the front door. As soon as he walked into Matthew's room, I broke down again. Aaron sat down and drew me into his arms, pressing his face onto my hair as I sobbed. Matthew kept asking, "Mama, you sad? Daddy, why Mama sad? Daddy sad, too?" Aaron tried to explain to him why we were both sad, but at three he was too young to really understand. We had not yet told him we were going to have a baby, and the "we were going to, and now we're not" conversation didn't make much sense to him. He only knew that the adults in his world were sad, and that was enough for him to declare, "I sad, too!"

Aaron had the hard job of calling both families that night, and no one really knew what to say. No one had expected us to get pregnant again so soon, which made this even more of a shock to them. His twelve-year-old sister said she was going to have a talk with God and give Him a piece of her mind. Aaron also called Terri, who realized what he was going to say as soon as she heard his voice on the phone. Our joy had just shattered.

6

How was I going to get through the next few days? We were scheduled to sing in a Christmas concert on Saturday afternoon, and our annual Christmas party was to be held on Saturday night. We had a lot of things to focus on, but I was finding it hard to focus.

Terri came over the day after the ultrasound, while Aaron was at work, and spent the morning hanging out with me while the boys played. The world seemed surreal to me, foggy, empty. And yet the boys played with no knowledge that anything was wrong. I didn't feel like I was a good conversation companion that morning, but with Terri, I didn't need to be. Having been through a pregnancy loss herself, she understood. I didn't have to make any pretenses of being okay. She let me talk or cry as I needed, and sometimes we just sat in silence. Mostly she was just there; it made a huge difference not having to be alone.

Aaron's family sent us a flower arrangement that afternoon, with a sympathy card. It was a very sweet gesture, and I appreciated the recognition of our baby very much. I think it also was a way for them to try to deal with the helplessness they were feeling at being unable to do anything to make this time better for us.

The bleeding began to pick up on Saturday, and this time, it was much stronger. The flow was very heavy, and the cramps were some of the worst I had ever felt. I had trouble standing up straight. I wanted to curl up into a little ball and not move, for every movement made me want to double over, but we had a concert to sing in and a house full of people coming that night. Looking back, I probably should have canceled the engagements—no one would have blamed us if we had. But at the time, it did not even occur to either of us to do so. Since we didn't really know what to do, we did what was on our calendar.

I spoke with Donna to ask about what I could do to ease the symptoms. She told me to try not to take too much Advil, since relieving the cramps would only slow the whole process down—but at the same time, to take as much as I needed to get through the concert and our party that night. Because she was concerned about how my body had dealt with this process the last time, she offered to put me on the schedule with Dr. Wolanski for a D&C on Wednesday. But I had a three-year old to think about. I couldn't have surgery three days before Christmas. Not unless it was absolutely necessary. And I really wanted to avoid surgery, if possible. She understood how I felt but she was still concerned. She said she would let it go until the following Monday, after Christmas; but if the blood work showed that things were not resolving, we would not wait any longer for surgery. We were not going to repeat what happened last time. Okay, I agreed. That makes sense.

Singing in the concert was physically difficult. Singing takes a lot of energy, and I had to be on my feet for most of the concert. I felt very detached from it, almost like I was watching someone else singing. The Christmas songs filled with joy at the coming of the Lord seemed hollow to me. It didn't feel like Christmas. The Advil wasn't taking the cramps completely away, and it began to wear off as the concert came to a close. I was feeling lousy by the time it was over. All I wanted to do was sleep. Two friends who were coming to the party that night were also singing in the concert, and after it was over, we shared our news with them and asked if they would be willing to come over a little early to give us a hand in getting ready. I took a nap while Aaron cleaned, then took another large dose of Advil before our friends arrived to help with setting up. We went through our party trying to be as friendly and cheerful as usual—whether anyone guessed something was wrong, I'll never know. It just didn't seem to be the time or the place to say anything.

At one point during the evening, Matthew was holding Margaret, the three-month-old daughter of our friend Brian, who had been with us when we wrote Joshua's name in the book at church. I overheard his wife, Audrey, say, "Matthew, you are going to be such a good big brother!" She didn't know what was going on, and in my living room full of people, it wasn't the time to tell her. But it was all I could do to keep from crying. All I could think was, "Yeah, if he ever gets the chance."

As I look back on that weekend, I wonder why it didn't occur to us to cancel our commitments in order to focus on what was happening in our family. Physically, I dragged myself through two draining events in one day. If anyone had known I was in the process of a miscarriage, they would have told me to forget about singing and go straight to bed. Our friends would probably have been shocked if they knew we were hosting a party in the middle of this loss. And yet, it never even crossed my mind to back out. It was not a conscious decision that we made, to focus on other things outside of our loss. We never even talked about it. We just went on with our schedule. From the vantage point of more than ten years later, I can see that for many reasons, it was just easier to go ahead with scheduled plans. It was something to do. We were both feeling lost in a fog, and following routines was the easiest way to keep moving forward. Perhaps Donna knew that also, for even she did not suggest we think about canceling our plans, but gave me permission to take as much Advil as was needed to get through it all. It baffles me now, to wonder why we went through with those events, for if faced with the same thing at this point in my life, I would definitely put myself and my body's needs first. But at the time, the feelings of being on auto pilot definitely prevailed.

7

The emotional impact of this miscarriage hit Aaron fully. There were a number of times in the first few days when his eyes would tear up, though I never saw him cry. I didn't want him to be hurting, but it made a big difference to me to know I was not alone in this. One night out of the blue, he suddenly said to me, "I'm sorry for last time. Now I understand what you went through. I know it wasn't my fault, but now I know how you must have felt, and I'm really sorry that you had to go through it alone." It meant so much to me to hear him say that. As hard as it was to be going through this again, at least this time it was our sorrow to bear.

Two days before Christmas, I called Donna to tell her I thought I had passed the embryo. I had been to the bathroom and after wiping, noticed a small gray mass, about the size of the first joint of my thumb on toilet paper. It was shaped rather like a cashew nut, and had a darker spot on the larger section that looked all for the world like an eye. Yes, Donna agreed, that was the embryo. The cramps had intensified in the few hours before, and she said since the cervix would need to dilate to about 2-3 cm in order for the embryo to pass, the cramps were an indication that the miscarriage was progressing. That was good, for the more my body appeared to be taking care of things by itself, the less likely it was that I would need surgery again. But she made me promise I would still go in to Martha Jefferson for the blood draw on

Monday.

Passing the embryo gave me a feeling of deja vu, and I began to remember the experience I had had after Matthew was born. I had never seen anything like this except for that time, which got me wondering about it again. But I didn't mention that to anyone.

My family came down on Christmas Eve, as usual, and I put a lot of energy into making Christmas a happy time, especially for Matthew. I focused on getting the things done that needed to be done. My mother commented to me that I seemed to be doing fine, as if the loss of this baby wasn't upsetting me. I looked her in the eye and said, "That's because I've shut it all off." The few days following Christmas were much harder. I only had so much emotional energy, and it went into making Matthew's Christmas a special time. It left me exhausted—a combination of physical and emotional drain. My mother pointed out that I had been doing too much over those few days, and she was probably right. I was still in the midst of a miscarriage, after all.

The Sunday after Christmas our friend Brian slid into the pew next to me during the opening song. As we sat down, he enveloped Matthew and me into a sideways hug. He had that "I wish I could say something to make it go away" look in his eyes, so I knew he was aware of what had happened.

"Sharon told you," I said.

He nodded. "Audrey and I cried a lot."

After mass, he gave Aaron a hug, one father to another. He told us that our mutual friend Sharon, a member of my prayer group, had called to tell them and had cried on the phone. His wife, Audrey, had figured out what had happened from hearing Brian's end of the conversation. Terri had emailed the prayer group so I wouldn't have to tell everyone myself, and slowly the news was spreading to other friends. It was comforting to have others grieving with and for us this time. Though there was nothing anyone could do to make it any better, it helped me to know that others were hurting for us.

Our friends had been very supportive the last time, but I had still felt so alone. I didn't feel that way now.

This experience was much more traumatic than what we went through with Joshua. That had been very hard, but it had been surreal since I had never had confirmation of being pregnant until it was over. The last time, my body seemed to want to hang on to the pregnancy; this time it seemed to want to purge itself of the child as quickly as possible. With Joshua, I had never had cramps and pain, just a light bleeding that didn't go away. It had taken a long time to come to terms with what was happening and how to refer to it both to myself and to others. This time, we'd had the positive test and blood work, and everything seemed to be going well. Intellectually, I knew that there was probably something wrong with this baby, but that didn't stop my emotions from screaming, "I want my baby back!" The suddenness of it all was like a waking nightmare: it couldn't possibly be my life we're talking about. Could it? But on the day we went for the ultrasound, part of me knew, deep down, that this baby had already died.

I knew we needed to choose a name for this baby, but I was just not ready to face that yet. Aaron and I both had strong feelings that this baby had been a girl, but it was just too raw to begin to go through the name book again.

The final blood work drawn on the Monday after Christmas showed a pregnancy hormone level of 5. A level of 2 or below is considered not pregnant. However, since the numbers had been up in the 400's the previous week, Donna considered this test to be negative. Most likely, she told me, there was just a little residual hormone left in my system. At least we would be able to avoid the surgery. My body had been much more efficient this time, but I felt like a sponge that had been wrung out. Where just a week ago I had been filled with excitement and love for this new little member of our family, now I was battered and empty.

The sense of fear was overpowering. How am I ever going

to face the possibility of getting pregnant again? Donna said that this miscarriage didn't indicate a problem, since we carried Matthew to term with no difficulties. Perhaps it was just "really bad luck." Give yourself some time, she counseled. Let your body and your heart have some time to heal before you deal with the next step. But I had a feeling that the fear would be much harder to overcome next time.

8

When Matthew was first born, I used to have the feeling that, someday, I would have to face the experience of losing a baby. Now, however, I was having recurrent thinking about the number three. Every time I would think, "Now I have two babies in Heaven," a little voice would whisper, "No, there are three." Did that mean that I would have to go through another miscarriage at some point? I wasn't sure my heart could withstand that. I began thinking back to the time after Matthew was born, realizing that what I had experienced then was the same as I had just gone through. Did this feeling mean that small gray mass really was a lost baby, and I already had three children in Heaven? Or was I just losing my mind completely?

Part of me still didn't believe it was real, even after all the physical discomfort I had felt. As we slowly shared our news with friends, I would hear myself say, "We lost another baby." But, as before, the words sounded as if they came from a bad dream. And no one knew what to say in response. There wasn't much anyone could say. No words were going to take the pain away. Friends gave us hugs, and prayers and were sad for us, but no one could take this burden from us. My heart felt like it was broken in pieces.

Matthew's godfather told me that he thought this was the most difficult thing I would ever have to face. He said he couldn't think of anything worse for me, someone who had always felt so called to be a mother, than losing a child. If you can survive this, he told me, you can survive anything. I hoped he was right.

As the holidays ended, Matthew continued to ask if we were going to have a baby soon. When we reminded him that the baby had died, he asked, "Why? Why did the baby die?" Oh, little one, if only we had an answer for you! One night when some friends were visiting, he asked this question yet again. When I told him I didn't know why the baby had died, he proceeded to poll all the adults at the table, one by one. "Why, Aunt Missy? Why did the baby die?" Surely someone could give him an answer—don't adults know everything? He was definitely trying to process this in his own way. But the concrete answers he was seeking were not there. When Matthew returned to his preschool after the Christmas break, I informed his teacher what had happened, just in case he shared his questions with the other adults in his world. He frequently talked of being a big brother, and it made my heart ache to hear him so ready.

The emotional impact of this miscarriage was much stronger than with Joshua. This time, for both Aaron and me, there was a deep feeling of loss. Having had the confirmation that I was pregnant and anticipating the joy of sharing that news, we had been confident all would be well with this pregnancy. After all, lightning doesn't strike twice, right? Now my body felt bereft of the pregnancy symptoms and my heart felt as if a piece had been taken out of it. Where the love for this new member of our family had been growing, now there was just emptiness. Some days I found I could talk with my emotions in check. My mother-in-law would call to see how we were doing, and I could honestly say I was okay. My emotions were stable and, though my heart still hurt, I was moving through my daily routines as usual. Other days When Matthew was first born, I used to have the feeling that, someday, I would have to face the experience of losing a baby. Now, however, I was having recurrent thinking about the number three. Every time I would think, "Now I have two babies in Heaven," a little voice would whisper, "No, there are three." Did that mean that I would have to go through another miscarriage at some point? I wasn't sure my heart could withstand that. I began thinking back to the time after Matthew was born, realizing that what I had experienced then was the same as I had just gone through. Did this feeling mean that small gray mass really was a lost baby, and I already had three children in Heaven? Or was I just losing my mind completely?

Part of me still didn't believe it was real, even after all the physical discomfort I had felt. As we slowly shared our news with friends, I would hear myself say, "We lost another baby." But, as before, the words sounded as if they came from a bad dream. And no one knew what to say in response. There wasn't much anyone could say. No words were going to take the pain away. Friends gave us hugs, and prayers and were sad for us, but no one could take this burden from us. My heart felt like it was broken in pieces.

Matthew's godfather told me that he thought this was the most difficult thing I would ever have to face. He said he couldn't think of anything worse for me, someone who had always felt so called to be a mother, than losing a child. If you can survive this, he told me, you can survive anything. I hoped he was right.

As the holidays ended, Matthew continued to ask if we were going to have a baby soon. When we reminded him that the baby had died, he asked, "Why? Why did the baby die?" Oh, little one, if only we had an answer for you! One night when some friends were visiting, he asked this question yet again. When I told him I didn't know why the baby had died, he proceeded to poll all the adults at the table, one by one. "Why, Aunt Missy? Why did the baby die?" Surely someone could give him an answer—don't adults know everything? He was definitely trying to process this in his own way. But the concrete answers he was seeking were not there. When

Matthew returned to his preschool after the Christmas break, I informed his teacher what had happened, just in case he shared his questions with the other adults in his world. He frequently talked of being a big brother, and it made my heart ache to hear him so ready.

The emotional impact of this miscarriage was much stronger than with Joshua. This time, for both Aaron and me, there was a deep feeling of loss. Having had the confirmation that I was pregnant and anticipating the joy of sharing that news, we had been confident all would be well with this pregnancy. After all, lightning doesn't strike twice, right? Now my body felt bereft of the pregnancy symptoms and my heart felt as if a piece had been taken out of it. Where the love for this new member of our family had been growing, now there was just emptiness. Some days I found I could talk with my emotions in check. My mother-in-law would call to see how we were doing, and I could honestly say I was okay. My emotions were stable and, though my heart still hurt, I was moving through my daily routines as usual. Other days were very tough emotionally, and it was all I could do to keep my tears back all day long. There was no way to tell how a day was going to go, and there was nothing I could do to change it. It was just the way things were.

There are three couples among our group of friends with whom we routinely got together for dinner and a board game. In early January, we got together at Sharon and Ken's house. We had talked to or seen both Brian and Audrey and Sharon and Ken over the holidays, but Mary Jo and Aiden had been away visiting family, so no one had seen them to tell them of our news. Suddenly, in the middle of the evening, Aiden announced that they were expecting their second child. Both of the other couples glanced at me and Aaron, unsure of how to react to this news. After several long seconds, Audrey finally put on an overly cheerful face and said, "Wow, that's great!"

I'm sure Mary Jo and Aiden were confused as to why the

group's reaction was so subdued, and I felt awful that they did not receive the kind of response they deserved, for truly we all were happy for them. It would have been too awkward to tell them what had happened after that announcement, but I struggled to keep my face neutral and keep from crying. Shortly after Aiden's announcement, I took refuge in the kitchen on the pretense of refilling my water glass. Sharon came in after me and gave me a hug. She had had no idea that that kind of announcement was coming, or she would have made sure to talk to Mary Jo before everyone came over. I knew that they had not been told about our situation, and if they had known they probably would not have said anything, but it was really not what I needed to hear right then.

When Sharon spoke to Mary Jo the next day and mentioned that we all felt bad as to the lack of response to their announcement, Mary Jo said she had been concerned about how I would react because of our difficult experience in the fall. Sharon assured her that I would have been fine with that, but "they just lost another one two weeks ago." Mary Jo felt awful and said they never would have said anything if they had known. We all knew that. There was no fault on anyone's part—just really lousy timing.

Sharon and I met for lunch one day in mid-January, and she gave me a gift—a cross-stitch of Jesus holding children in His arms, with a quote from the Gospel of Matthew: "Let the little children come to me." She said she had wanted to help in some way, and there was nothing she could do, so she made this keepsake in memory of our babies. She had found the pattern in a book during the autumn and decided to make it because she needed a project to work on, figuring she would find someone to give it to later. After she found out about our second loss, she told Ken, "Now I know who I am doing it for."

When I brought it home and showed it to Aaron, he immediately commented that he thought it was interesting that there were three children in the picture. I hadn't focused on that when I unwrapped it the first time. Aaron and I had discussed the connection between this most recent loss and what I had experienced after Matthew was born. The more I had thought about it, the more I had been feeling certain that we really did have three babies in Heaven, two boys and a girl. The children in the picture were two boys and a girl.

I called Sharon to tell her about the feelings I had been having of there really being three. She found that very interesting, for when she was working on it, it had seemed perfect except for there being three children. Because she hadn't wanted me to feel there might be another loss yet to come she had considered taking one of them out, but something made her leave it in. I told her that I saw the hand of God at work in this, and she agreed. She also saw two boys and a girl.

I had been asking God if there was a way to know, to come to a sense of peace about this feeling of having lost three children. Was Sharon's gift my answer? I shared my thoughts with Sr. Pat one day, and she too saw the hand of God at work. Yes, she believed that this was God's answer: God worked through Sharon to confirm that there had indeed been two heartbeats on that first prenatal visit four years ago. Seeing two boys and a girl in Sharon's needlework, both Aaron and I felt that our first baby had been a boy. This did not intensify our grief over this most recent miscarriage, since it had happened so long ago. But I decided as we looked for a name for this most recent baby, we would name the first one also.

We hung the picture in the hallway right outside of our bedroom, and looking at it brought me comfort. I was not over the raw feelings of grief, by any means, but when I looked at this picture, I could hear a quiet voice say, "They're here, I've got them. It's okay." Sharon's gift gave me the beginning of a sense of peace, for I could be peaceful knowing my children were in Heaven. But my heart continued to hurt. I missed them. How could my heart be so empty and so heavy at the same time?

The next week, I went for a check-up with Donna, to be sure my body had healed after the miscarriage. I told her that every time I thought I had this all under control, it would erupt again. It hasn't been long enough, she reminded me. These things take time. I realized she was right: it hadn't been all that long. It felt like so much longer than a month had passed.

We discussed whether there might be a hormonal component to these losses. She told me doctors don't usually pursue explanations until after a woman has had three miscarriages in a row. Two in a row is not considered by the medical field to be an indication of a problem. Technically, our situation was still just considered to be bad luck. All I could think was, You are kidding me, right? I'll have to go this nightmare again before you begin to investigate why it is happening? She agreed: that really stinks. Since there are some simple things that can be checked with blood work, Donna decided to order those tests now. If there was a hormonal problem, it could be corrected easily. If not, then we would know that there most likely had been something wrong with this most recent baby. Either way, it might relieve some of the apprehension about another pregnancy.

Donna also decided she wanted me to begin to chart my basal body temperature, taking my temperature each morning before I got out of bed, and plotting it on a graph. A woman's body temperature is usually about a half a degree warmer in the second half of the month, after ovulation has occurred, as the progesterone levels rise in preparation for a potential pregnancy. Charting my temperature changes would give her the most information about what my hormones were doing throughout the month, especially the progesterone levels. If the progesterone drops, then even a healthy embryo cannot maintain its implantation in the uterus, and a miscarriage occurs. Donna said it would be best to have at least three months of charts to compare, and we decided I would see her again in April to review them. She also recommended that we wait until we had that information before conceiving again, which was fine with me. I was not even close to being ready to get pregnant again.

At the end of January, my prayer group began meeting again after a long holiday break. One of our members had delivered her baby eight weeks prematurely in December, and we had put off the baby shower for her until the baby was close to coming home. After several complications that kept the baby in hospital longer than expected, she was finally almost ready to come home. I began to dread going to this shower. Another one of our members had just told us she was pregnant, and I knew it was going to be very hard to be around both of them. Genevieve had been thoughtful enough to talk to Terri first and ask her to tell me about her pregnancy so that I would not have to hear it for the first time at a meeting. But she was due right around the time that I should have delivered, and I knew it wasn't going to be easy to watch her pregnancy progress. At the same time, I couldn't hide myself from expectant friends and new moms. So I forced myself to attend the shower, even though Terri told me I didn't have to go. She had had to face similar situations after her baby had died, and she cautioned me that I could find it very difficult to be surrounded by baby things. I knew she was probably right, but I also couldn't think of a way to back out of it. Sometimes, I decided, you just have to force yourself to go through hard situations as part of the healing process. Terri offered to leave with me, if it got too hard for me to stay.

Though I had gotten a few emails and cards from members of the group after Terri had told them of our loss, this was the first time we were meeting together since the miscarriage. Perhaps it was because the focus was on the new mom, but no mention was made of our loss. No one but Terri seemed to realize how hard it was for me to be there. And we did leave early, as soon as it would not be considered rude to do so. I had to escape the talk about babies.

I began to feel as if I was never going to feel happy again. My arms and heart ached to hold the babies I would never see. Donna had reminded me that it hadn't been all that long and that healing takes time. How much time? I began to wonder if perhaps we had gotten pregnant again too soon. Had I completely healed from Joshua? I didn't think we had rushed things. I had felt ready to try again, but perhaps the short amount of time between these two losses was making things worse.

9

By the end of January, I was feeling like a big jumbled mess. Strong emotions were all mixed up together, and I was beginning to think I would never find a way out of them. I was not used to crying easily or getting angry over things without reason. I was well aware that anger is a very normal part of the grief process. The anger needs to come out somehow, but at what? I could be angry at the situation, but that didn't really do me any good. I found it was coming out at other people and at things that had nothing to do with my situation. Fortunately, I recognized this tendency and was able to keep myself from saying inappropriate things to other people. I was really not angry at my friends who were pregnant, or not being included in something, or at God. I was angry that my life had changed so drastically and was totally beyond my control. I knew that the only thing that was going to make this better was the passage of time. But it is so hard to feel bad and want to feel better and not be able to do anything to control that process.

One of the books I read used an image of a potter's wheel and a person being a lump of clay that God was molding and forming. In discussing that image with a friend of mine, she said she thought of herself as a fired piece that needed to be shattered before it could be reworked. I have never considered myself to be a finished piece; I have too many flaws that still need to be fixed. Right now, I just felt like a jumbled, squishy mess of clay, a piece that had been molded, then squashed—not only formless and shapeless, but without something beautiful inside. I knew I should let go and let God do the reworking, but God works on His time, not ours. And waiting to feel better on someone else's schedule was hard.

I felt I was not handling anything in my life well, most especially motherhood.

Matthew was engaging in the normal, trying-to-push-the-limits-behavior of a three-year-old. But I found myself much more impatient with him than I should have been, much quicker to snap at him for age-appropriate behaviors. I felt awful about taking my emotional state out on him; it wasn't his fault. But three-year-olds require so much patience, and patience takes emotional energy. I just didn't have any extra.

Terri was trying hard to be supportive of me, letting me talk or cry when I felt the need. My other friends had never been through the loss of a baby, and they didn't really know what to do for me. Terri understood. And yet, she told me she felt as if there wasn't much she could do to help, since she couldn't imagine having to go through this nightmare more than once. And here I had been feeling I was leaning on her too much!

People often don't know what to say to others who are grieving, and sometimes, though they mean well, they say things that do not help. Several people had tried to offer me condolences by telling me "This was God's will." I had a hard time with the idea that God had "done this" to me, for that just doesn't match my image of a loving God. I just couldn't see a loving God allowing a new life to form and then taking it away again on purpose. Sure, we're not allowed to choose our burdens, for who would ever choose most of them? But neither do I feel that God inflicts sufferings upon people. Life happens, and there are burdens we must bear. It is how we bear them that makes the difference.

Another friend told me that God provides the grace and help we need to get through difficult situations. I could take comfort in God providing the help we needed. He had certainly provided us with a lot of support. Perhaps I would feel the grace at some point on this journey.

Over the past two years, Aaron and I had done two musical productions with a local community theater near our home. Fiddler on the Roof, the previous spring, had been great fun, and the theater was getting ready to hold auditions for Oklahoma!, one of my favorite musicals. I decided I needed something to do to try and take my mind off the past few months. Theater seemed just the thing. Aaron and I were both cast in the show, and for the rest of the winter, I had a distraction in the evenings. Learning music and blocking gave me a reason to focus outside of myself, at least for a few hours each night. It is easier to appear normal when you are surrounded by other people. But my days remained a struggle.

I had made plans to go to DC for a baby shower for a life-long friend of mine, and as it drew near I found myself feeling like I needed to gather strength to face another shower. The mother-to-be had been my friend since we were babies and I didn't want to miss it. She had lost two pregnancies before carrying this one to term, and there was much to celebrate for this baby. And yet, I knew it would be hard. Shortly before the shower, my friend sent me an email in which she told me that, as much as she wanted me to be there, to please not feel like I had to force myself to come if it was going to be too hard for me. She knew from experience how wrenching such functions could be while grieving a loss, and she did not want me to have to suffer through the party if I felt I could not handle it. No, I wrote back. I want to be there. I'll be okay. Just knowing she understood that it would be hard and gave me the option out gave me the strength to attend. And I looked at her joy in carrying this baby to term after two losses with hope—perhaps we, too, would have something to celebrate after all this sorrow.

The discussion at prayer group one week turned to the

topic of trust: trusting in God completely. I knew that I needed to do just that if I was ever going to get through another pregnancy, but the fear was still so overpowering. Can you trust God completely and still be afraid? Sharon said that it is what you do with the fear that matters. If you let it keep you from doing something, then you are not fully trusting in God. Sometimes trusting fully in God is so hard. My arms still longed to hold my babies, and my heart was feeling very fragile—could I possibly expose it to that vulnerability again? The hills and valleys of day-to-day life were slowly smoothing out. The highs and lows were not as extreme as they had been a month before. But my heart still felt too raw to think of getting pregnant again.

By early March, I was feeling as if we could finally begin to think about naming our babies. Aaron and I each went through our baby name book and made a list of favorites. We had put so much thought into the meaning of Joshua's name, and I felt that meaning should play a role with naming our daughter as well. Aaron had been thinking of her as Victoria since we had lost her, so his list of choices was fairly short, but I was unsure. Sr. Pat said that Victoria means "victorious in Christ," but that just didn't seem to fit our situation. My choice was Elizabeth Noel: Elizabeth means "consecrated to God," and Noel is French for Christmas. But perhaps I should let Aaron name this baby since he felt connected this time. Perhaps Victoria Elizabeth Noel? Aaron vetoed that; it was too long. I pointed out to him that we'd never have to use it to call her in for dinner. In the end, we decided to give her all three names: Victoria Elizabeth Noel.

We then shifted our focus to the boys' names. We both felt that his middle name should be Thomas, which means twin. We quickly chose Zachary for the first name, which means "God remembered."

As the weeks went on, I had many conversations with Matthew in which he would wonder when he would get the chance to be a big brother. It hurt so much to hear him say that, for he so wanted to be one. One day while we were driving in the car and having one of those conversations, I told him he already was a big brother to our three babies in Heaven. He thought about that for a few moments and then said,

"I hope God is taking good care of them."

"I think so," I replied.

"God is playing the organ for them. But the babies aren't singing."

"Are they listening?" I asked.

"Yes. And the guitar players are playing, and they are singing to the babies."

"Are the angels singing to them?" I wondered.

"Yes. And playing a quiet drum and quiet cymbals and a banjo and a quiet trumpet. Because babies don't like loud sounds. It makes them cry. So they are playing quiet."

After a few moments of silence, he continued,

"God is cooking them dinner."

"He feeds them?" I asked.

"Yes... They are okay up in Heaven. God hugs them and kisses them."

How easily the young can take comfort in such thoughts! If only it were so easy for me. If I agree that they are safe and in a good place and that God is taking care of them, why can't my heart let them go?

10

In April, Aaron and I cashed in some frequent flier miles and traveled to Italy for a week. The past six months had been difficult for both of us, and we felt we needed some time away as a couple. Even though *Oklahoma!* had been a very good distraction, it had cut into our personal time quite a bit. We had been together every evening at rehearsals, but had had very little time to spend as a couple. Aaron's mother, Mary, came and took care of Matthew, and we spent eight days exploring a small part of northern Italy and reconnecting with each other. The gap between us that had been so large following Joshua's death had narrowed a great deal. But Victoria's death had brought new stresses and pain, and though we were much closer than we had been a few months earlier, the holidays, the show, and our three-year-old had not given us much time to heal.

One day, in a small town on Lake Como, we stepped into a little shop to escape the rain. While Aaron was looking at leather bookmarks, deciding on which to add to his collection, I began browsing the figurines in a case along the counter. Many of them were Christmas ornaments, and among them I discovered a small carved wooden angel, a little girl with brown hair, holding a small evergreen tree. I knew immediately that we had found an angel ornament for Victoria. The fact that we had found it on the trip that was prompted by her loss made it even more special.

Though the trip lasted only a week, the time without any other obligations did wonders for me, and I returned home feeling more like myself than I had in months. I did not feel that it was all behind me, and I was still not ready to face another pregnancy. I knew I must let go of the fear first, and that daunted me. But I was beginning to think about it.

The feelings of stability diminished during the third week of April, the time Joshua should have been due. Chris had been right to tell me not to be alone. The sadness came back, almost as strong as it had been after my surgery. My breasts ached, as if they knew they were supposed to be nourishing a new life, and my arms could almost feel the weight of the bundle they didn't cuddle. I should have also been anticipating his sister, feeling her move for the first time. If that were true, maybe I wouldn't miss him so much. But Victoria was gone also. There was nothing but emptiness where my children should have been. It didn't help that good friends of ours called to tell us they were expecting again. I could tell by Aaron's end of the conversation why they were calling, and I managed to convey to him nonverbally that I did not want to get on the phone. I know they did not realize the significance of that week, but the news cut like a knife on an already tender heart. I couldn't congratulate them right then. When Aaron got off the phone, I let the tears flow. Why did it seem like everyone else was having no trouble having children? It wasn't fair.

The feelings that reared up so strongly that week ebbed back quickly once we got passed Joshua's expected time, and the feelings of stability that had come with our time in Italy returned. I was surprised at the intensity with which the sorrow had returned, but also with how quickly the pain reverted to an ache. I knew from my reading that the grief process is a spiral and you pass through the stages over and over again. As the journey of healing continues, each pass through the hard stages will be shorter and less intense. This pass, though intense, was brief, and localize around a specific, significant point in time. The rapidity with which the calmer feelings returned told me I was moving along the path of healing.

After our trip, I went back for another discussion with Donna. The blood work had come back normal, which was a good thing. There were no serious problems with my thyroid or other rare causes of miscarriage. But there were no answers, either. The temperature charts were looking okay, staying up for close to the right amount of time. The second half of the cycle, the ludial phase, should have temperatures staying a half a degree or more above the first half for at least 14 days. Most months it was only up for 12-13, and she was okay with that, but at the same time, the temperatures were not elevated consistently during the second half of the month —they fluctuated. And one month it remained elevated for only 10 days, which was way too short. Donna decided we should treat this as a progesterone deficiency, even if it was not an obvious one. She would treat me with progesterone during the next pregnancy, just to be on the safe side.

Progesterone is often administered through shots or oral medications, but since my problem did not appear to be a severe deficiency, we would use a topical cream instead. The small amount of cream rubbed onto the skin of my inner thigh several times a day should provide enough extra progesterone to even out the hormone level in the second half of the month. If that was the cause of the miscarriages, then it should solve the problem. And if it was not a factor, the extra progesterone would not be harmful to the pregnancy or to the development of the baby. My body would ignore what it did not need. There were no guarantees that it would help, of course, but at least we would be able to rule out progesterone deficiency as the problem.

Looking at the graphs more closely, I began to see a pattern between the ovulations on my left and right sides. On months when ovulation happened from the right ovary, I would experience a cramping feeling around the mid-point of the cycle. I would not feel that on the alternate months, when ovulation happened on the left. The graphs for the months when I ovulated from the left ovary looked the same, and the graphs for the right ovary looked the same. But they did not resemble each other. Calculating back, I was pretty sure that both Joshua and Victoria had been conceived during left-side months. Could there be a problem with my left ovary?

Donna agreed that could be part of the problem. Perhaps the ovary on the left side had been through a trauma of some kind—something as benign as a ball hitting me in the abdomen too hard as a child. Perhaps that ovary never developed properly, and the eggs in it were not as healthy. There was no way to tell for sure. However, she felt that without other conclusive reasons for the miscarriages, suspicions like that should not be ignored. If the left-side ovary was potentially the problem, we should probably err on the side of caution and limit the months we tried to conceive to those we knew would be right-side months.

I told Donna about Zachary and asked her if she remembered our conversation on the phone after Matthew was born, when I told her about the small gray mass I had passed. She did. She had suspected a twin at the time, but felt it was not something I needed to hear right then. Theoretically, my body should have reabsorbed the deceased embryo long before Matthew was born. It was very unusual that we should know about Zachary at all. Donna said she thought God wanted us to know he was there, which is what Aaron and I had been feeling, and the reason we named him as we did. Donna wrote both Zachary's and Victoria's names in my chart—Joshua's was already there. It made me feel good to see her recognize these children in print. Their lives may have been short, but they were important.

Now Aaron and I had an important decision to make. The next cycle, in only a few weeks' time, should be a right-side month. Should we try to conceive? Was I really ready? It seemed almost rushing things, but at the same time, waiting several more months seemed a long time. Aaron was ready, but he knew that I needed to feel sure. I was longing to have another baby, but the fear still loomed. I knew I would never have another pregnancy like Matthew's, to enjoy without any worry. I could not see myself ever letting go of the fear fully. Aaron told me it was my decision, and we would wait until I felt fully prepared. I finally decided that I was never going to feel 100 percent ready: the fear was never going to be fully gone. We decided to go ahead.

11

In mid-June, I saw Donna for my annual exam. She looked at my charts and then at me with a raised eyebrow. "Are you pregnant?"

"I don't know," I replied. It was just around the time that my cycle should be starting, but it had not yet.

"Well, let's find out." She handed me a pregnancy test and told me to leave it on the edge of the sink in the bathroom. When I had changed for my exam, I sat nervously swinging my feet off the edge of the exam table. Donna came back into the room with the test stick in her hand and silently showed me two pink lines. I let out the breath I didn't realize I had been holding, closed my eyes for a moment, then looked her in the eye. She gave me a hug and said, "Let's hope this one takes."

"From your mouth to God's ears," I replied, quoting what my grandmother used to say when someone voiced an urgent wish or a prayer.

I wished I could be overjoyed at the news we were expecting, dancing and exited as I should be. I was thrilled we had conceived easily, but I was also filled with trepidation. We were only at four weeks. The journey ahead of me seemed very long, like a tall mountain of which I could not see the top. We had still had several weeks to go before we would pass the point at which I had miscarried the last two pregnancies. Even when we passed that point, Donna cautioned, we would not really start to relax until we reached the end of the first trimester, at twelve weeks. After that, the odds of losing a pregnancy drop drastically. Eight weeks before we reached that point. It seems so far away, I told her. Donna nodded. She patted my hand as I lay back for my exam. "One day at a time."

She started me on the progesterone cream that day, once in the morning and once at night, and said we would run some blood work and then do an ultrasound in a few weeks to confirm that everything was as it should be. Although she did not completely restrict my activities, Donna did forbid me from lifting anything over ten pounds or engaging in strenuous exercise. We weren't going to take any risks with this pregnancy.

After my exam, Donna came out into the waiting room with me. Aaron had been watching Matthew in the play area during my appointment. She walked over and offered her hand. He shook it, then looked at me and asked if we had news. I just smiled.

We told Matthew at dinner that night. Even though we knew it was going to be a very long time for him to wait, we felt it was important for him to know right away, before we told anyone else. We had not done that the past two times, thinking he was too young to really understand. But he was a bit older now, and we wanted this wait to be as a family. Also, Matthew would understand why I was not allowed to carry him or why I was feeling tired. We had been telling him that he would have a baby brother or sister when God said it was the right time. When we told him I was pregnant, he said, "Did God say yes?!" I hoped so.

We were happy, of course, but knew we faced a long road ahead. Although two miscarriages in a row did not technically constitute a medical problem, the risks of losing the next pregnancy increased to about 40 percent. There was nothing we could do but take it one day at a time and place this baby in God's care.

We called our families even though it was so early. Many people will chose to wait until the end of the first trimester to tell people they are pregnant, as we had done with Matthew. However, our families had never known we were expecting until we weren't the last two times, and I think it made it hard for them to relate to what was happening. I couldn't stand the thought of having to tell people after the fact again, if something happened this time, and I needed as many people as possible praying for this baby. Many times in my life I had seen positive answers to prayers asked by a community: friends healed from advanced diseases, successful outcomes of complicated surgeries. And the people for whom others were praying always said they could feel the love and support of those who were praying. I needed that support to try and keep the fear away. As we shared the news with more people, I had the feeling of a web being woven around me and the baby, many arms, many prayers, weaving together to support and protect us both.

I tried very hard to just live each day and not be afraid.

Some days, the fear of losing this baby would flood to the surface. This was raw panic, like the seconds before your car is about to be hit from behind. It was particularly bad as we entered week six, the point at which we had lost the last two pregnancies. I asked Terri about the days of panic—are these normal? If so, how do you get through them? There will be those days, she told me, all the way through until you have that baby safely in your arms. And there isn't much you can do about them; you just have to ride them out. Put it in God's hands and try to let Him carry that anxiety for you, she counseled. But it won't be easy.

I was beginning to feel...yucky. With Matthew I had been queasy, but if I ate only bland things, like bagels and crackers, I was usually okay. This time, I felt on the verge of throwing up all day long. I never got sick, but the thought of eating was not a pleasant one. I managed to eat oyster crackers and drink ginger ale, but not much else, it seemed. It was hard to care for Matthew, and the poor kid spent a lot of time listening to books that I read while lying on the sofa. I realized that every pregnancy is different, but I wondered if the extra progesterone could be making these symptoms worse. Then again, feeling sick was a good thing, for every day I felt awful meant that I was still pregnant. And that was the only thing we had to go on at that point.

At seven and a half weeks, we went in for the ultrasound. Aaron went with me to the hospital—I could not face this test alone. I had never had an ultrasound done with Matthew, so my only experience was the day we found out Victoria had died. I was quite nervous going into the exam room—what if they couldn't find the heartbeat this time? As we sat waiting, I silently prayed over and over, "Please let things be okay, please let things be okay." I gripped Aaron's hand while the gel was spread on my abdomen, and I watched his face instead of the screen. I saw him lean closer as I heard the technician say, "There you go." I turned to view the screen, and there was a rhythmic pulsing dot in the middle of the bean-sized embryo. A few tears escaped as I stared at the screen. Thank you, thank you, thank you, I thought. The technician proceeded to do measurements and assured us all was well. The baby was just the size it was supposed to be. We were overjoyed to hear that, but we knew we were still not out of the woods—there were still many weeks to go before we would move beyond the first trimester.

Even with the good ultrasound report, my fears continued to well up now and then. There were moments when it was all I could do to keep the tears at bay. I was walking on eggshells, half expecting to see bleeding every time I went to the bathroom. I knew we must put this baby in God's hands and trust that all would be well this time. But it seemed as if I was waiting for the proverbial second shoe to drop, anticipating sadness instead of joy. Would we really be allowed to keep this baby? I longed to feel the joys of expectant motherhood the way I had with Matthew, reading pregnancy books and looking at nursery items, blissfully dreaming of the softness of baby skin nestled on my shoulder. I couldn't let myself think that far ahead. The days seemed to go by so slowly. I felt as if I was still at the bottom of a very tall mountain, with a steep path to climb, and some days the journey up to the top seemed insurmountable.

As we got closer to the end of the first trimester, I began to have problems with insomnia. I would go to bed exhausted, then wake up around 1 am every night, and spend several hours trying to get back to sleep. After several nights of this, I finally got up and went into the living room to read, rather than watch the clock. Finally, around five in the morning, I would be able to sleep again, but only until Matthew would get up two hours later. I read lots of books over those few weeks, but the hours of being awake at night did nothing to help the fatigue I was feeling during the day. Was I going to feel like this for the next six months?

12

At our 11-week check-up, we heard the heartbeat for the first time. Fast and strong, there was no music that ever sounded sweeter. One more milestone down. I told Donna about the insomnia, and she decided that we could begin to wean me off the progesterone. The placenta should be doing most of the hormone support for the pregnancy at this point, and perhaps the added progesterone from the cream was contributing to the insomnia. She told me to continue to monitor my temperature, but to gradually decrease the usage of the cream. As I did, the insomnia and the nausea began to decrease, and once I was off the cream entirely, I was able to go back to sleeping through the night. Food began to taste better as my stomach calmed down, and my energy began to increase as I felt better each day.

As we got into August, we approached Victoria's due date. The week Joshua would have been due had been a very hard time and I was anticipating her due date being a rough day. However, despite my friend Genevieve being due any minute, it was not as bad as I expected. Perhaps that was because I was pregnant and almost through the most stressful time of the first trimester. At the end of April, around the time Joshua should have been due, there was the added grief for Victoria as well, which made that time so much worse.

As we passed the end of this first trimester, I was still struggling with fear, despite all indications pointing to a healthy pregnancy. I just couldn't seem to fully believe that all would be well with this baby. I asked Donna if we could do a 20-week ultrasound. She figured we wanted to know the gender of the baby, but I told her I didn't even want to be told that. I just needed to know this baby was okay. She agreed without further discussion.

In September we went back to Camp Trinity. The month of August had marked one year since we had lost Joshua, and the retreat marked a year since the grieving process had really begun. It was so hard to believe all that had happened in just one year. I tried to see that weekend as a time of healing, of putting the grief behind me. Many of the readings and songs used that weekend had the theme of God being in charge and of giving all things over to Him. The readers used the lilies of the field as one of the readings, which we had used as the gospel in our wedding:

> "Therefore do not worry about tomorrow,
> for tomorrow will worry about itself.
> Each day has enough trouble of its own."
> (Matthew 6:34).

The psalm we had used in our wedding was also sung that weekend:

> "You are all we have.
> You give us what we need.
> Our lives are in your hands, O Lord,
> our lives are in your hands"
> (Frances Patrick O'Brien).

I felt that God was trying to remind me of His promises. It was as if He was saying, "If you could put yourselves in My hands then, why can't you do it now?" I didn't feel as if I had ever gone away from that, really. I still believed we were in His hands, and I knew He would be there for us, whatever came. But I made a new commitment to putting this baby in His hands and trying not to let my human mother's heart worry too much.

As we got into the second trimester, the feeling of walking on eggshells began to ease somewhat. But around 15 weeks, my lower back began to hurt. I had not had any back problems with Matthew's pregnancy, and I thought this was awfully early to be experiencing them this time. Dr. Klas sent me for a physical therapy evaluation, and the therapist discovered that my pelvis was tilted up and rotated forward, which was putting strain on the muscles of my lower back.

As we were talking over what could have caused such a thing, I told her about the car accident we had had just before Matthew was born. Could it really have been a problem for four years that I didn't know about? When I described the nature of the accident, she felt that was the most likely explanation. It was the right side of my pelvis that was rotated and raised, which was consistent with the force of the impact coming from the back right corner of the car. She then told me I was lucky I had been pregnant at the time, for the hormones that cause everything to loosen up for delivery had allowed my pelvis to slide out of position easily instead of with force. If I had not been pregnant, I most likely would have sustained much more damage, with torn ligaments and possibly broken pelvic bones. I found it hard to believe that I had been walking around with this injury for four years and had not had a clue. At the time of the accident, my back did not hurt. And being pregnant for the first time, I had not been aware that the lower back ache I felt as Matthew's birth drew near was anything other than normal. Since then, I had felt the odd twinge in my back occasionally and had sometimes felt that something was not quite right, but as it had not caused me pain, I had never had it checked out. When I told Donna what was going on, she said it made all the back labor in Matthew's delivery make a lot more sense. If things are not aligned properly, the passage down is not an easy one.

But now, what could we do about it? The therapist assured me that we would be able to solve this problem and get the pelvis to remain stable, but not until after the baby was born.

As the baby continued to grow and gain weight, it was going to put more stress on the lower back and keep pulling the pelvis out of place. The best we could do was to keep pulling it back into alignment and wait until after the baby was born to retrain and strengthen the muscles. So I entered physical therapy twice a week for the remaining five months of the pregnancy.

Although I most likely would have had some restrictions placed on me in the healing process, the combination of the injury and the pregnancy made those restrictions mount. I had already been forbidden to pick up or carry Matthew, but now I was restricted from carrying groceries or laundry baskets and even from doing any other kind of housework. Most people would probably look at a get-out-of-housework-free card and rejoice, but the list of limitations began to frustrate me as the weeks progressed. And my energy level was low, which added to the frustrations—this was supposed to be the point at which I was feeling pretty good! My back tired easily, which led to a general fatigue, but the pain diminished with the therapy work. I spent a lot more time resting than I had during Matthew's pregnancy.

As we passed Thanksgiving, I came to realize that I really shouldn't look at the restrictions as a result of the pregnancy, for the baby was healthy and things were progressing very well. I needed to look at this time as healing from a four-year-old injury. My body was trying to do a lot at one time—grow a baby and heal an old injury. Of course, I was going to be tired. At least I was still up and around and not stuck in bed. My therapist told me that if we had not been working on trying to keep this in line every week, by the end of the third trimester I would not be able to walk. So I tried to keep my attitude a positive one.

As we passed into the new year, the due date at the end of February still seemed very far away. My fatigue was increasing, and I was beginning to doubt that I would have the strength for labor. I was feeling too physically drained.

Despite the fact that everyone tells you you forget what labor was like, my memories of all the horrendous back labor I had experienced with Matthew's delivery were very clear. Donna said that fears of labor with a first baby are fears of the unknown. Subsequent labors are fears of the known. I really wanted to have a drug-free delivery as I had done with Matthew, but I did not have the confidence in my ability to go though all of that again. How could I handle that kind of back labor when my back had already hurt so much through this pregnancy?

Aaron went with me to my physical therapist, and she taught him everything she could think of that might possibly help with my back during labor. Donna also had some ideas, and we agreed to do our best to manage this without medications, if possible.

At the beginning of February, Aaron dropped me off at my friend Peggy's house for a girl's afternoon of movie watching. Thinking it was just going to be me and Peggy's daughters, I walked into a room full of my friends and a surprise baby shower. Peggy had gathered friends from my prayer group and the theater—even my 85 year old friend Helen was there for the party. I was touched, but confused. People don't usually throw showers for a second baby. I already had all the baby stuff I needed from Matthew. Peggy could see my unspoken thought of "thank you, but why?" She gave me a big hug and said, "Because this baby needs to be celebrated."

Two weeks before my February 28th due date, I went for a check-up with Donna. She took one look at me as I walked back from the waiting room and could tell I was in pain. I told her I felt as if my bones themselves were hurting. My blood pressure was elevated, but since it is normally on the low side, it was now only in the normal range and Donna didn't seem too concerned about it. Most likely it was connected to the pain she could see on my face. She had told me it was okay to use Advil if I needed it, and she was a little concerned when I told her it was not helping at all. As she checked my measurements, she could tell that the baby was lower, and she decided to do an internal exam to find out where we stood. The baby was at zero station, as low as it could go and not have me in active labor. He or she was sitting right on the cervix, putting pressure on the pelvic bowl. So I was right, my bones were what was aching. Unfortunately, delivery was the only thing that was going to provide relief. Aaron was hoping for a February 29th delivery, since he thought 2/29/2000 would be a great birth date to have. But I wasn't sure I could deal with the pain much longer.

I was still so very tired, and everything was a major effort. Even getting up to get milk for Matthew at meals was exhausting. I had not gained very much weight in this pregnancy, only twenty-one pounds, which was a blessing. I couldn't imagine how my back would feel if I had also gained a lot of weight. I felt as if I was walking like a ninety-year-old arthritic woman, slowly and painfully. It was hard to stand very long, hard to sit very long—nothing was comfortable.

I wanted this baby's birth to be a positive thing, and not just something to be endured, but I beginning to feel doubtful. I was so tired that I didn't think I would have the energy to get through labor, though Donna assured me I would find it when I needed it. Where? I wondered.

I decided I needed to have something to focus on during labor. Childbirth classes often tell you to have a favorite object or photograph as your point of focus during contractions. But since I remembered mostly keeping my eyes closed during contractions with Matthew, I figured an object was not what I needed. I decided to use a psalm that we sing at church as a kind of mantra during contractions. Marty Haugen's arrangement of the 23rd Psalm, has always been one of my favorites. The words took on even more meaning for me at the end of this pregnancy:

"Shepherd me, O God,
beyond my wants,
Beyond my fears,
from death into life"

This pregnancy had been filled with fears and conquering them remained a struggle. Perhaps reciting the words to this prayer over and over would help.

On February 22nd, I was feeling not quite right, and I thought the odds were good that labor would begin soon. When Aaron came home from work that evening, I told him I was pretty sure we weren't going to make it to the 29th , as much as he was hoping we would. I rested that evening after dinner while Aaron put Matthew to bed. Contractions began around 9:30, but they were infrequent enough that I stayed in bed for a while more. By 11pm, however, I knew we were to be up for the rest of the night.

Around 3 am, Aaron called Peggy, who had agreed to take Matthew for us when we went to the hospital. I knew we were not quite ready to leave for Martha Jefferson, but I also did not want to have to drive in the opposite direction to drop Matthew off when the time came to go. Waking Matthew from a sound sleep has never been an easy task, but once Aaron said that the baby was coming, Matthew bounded out of bed. He looked so small going off in the middle of the night with his suitcase.

We had learned in our childbirth classes that walking can help speed up the labor. Because it was a very cold night, walking around the neighborhood was not very appealing. So I paced. I walked from the living room, down the hallway to the baby's room and back to the living room, over and over again. I began to feel like a caged animal. Aaron allowed me to pace, stepping up to rub my back when I would stop to lean on a wall for a contraction.

We spoke with Donna several times during the night, and she told me it was my decision when to come into the office. I really did not want to be at the hospital for as much time as we had spent with Matthew's labor, if we could avoid it. So I labored at home all night and went to Donna's office at 6:30 am, when I could no longer handle the back pain on my own.

I was dilated to 8 cm when we got to the hospital and was reaching the point where I could not breathe through the contractions. The pain was all around me this time, both in my abdominal muscles and in my back. But it was already too late for any medication to be of help. With a lot of massage and counter pressure along with a frequent change in positions, Donna and Aaron worked together to try and provide me some relief from the pain. Donna gave me injections of sterile water under the skin on my back, which helped to draw the nerve endings up and numb them, relieving some of the agony in my lower back. Hyperventilating became a problem again, just as it had been in Matthew's delivery. Only this time it was even worse. Where my fingers had been tingly in Matthew's labor, they now went completely stiff. Donna had to keep massaging them to get them to bend.

Because I had never felt the need to push in Matthew's delivery, Donna checked this baby's progress more frequently. Judging by my inability to control my breathing through the contractions and the level of pain I seemed to be experiencing, she finally made the decision to have me try pushing. Unfortunately, the sterile water injections wore off right as she got me into the bed. I could not focus, I could not breathe; all I wanted was to get away from the pain. Donna had the nurse and Aaron providing me support and, somehow, she managed to get me to focus on her face and put my energy into pushing. I had felt strong in pushing with Matthew's birth. This time, the pain did not go away with pushing, it intensified. All I wanted to do was curl up and cry. Twelve minutes after she had me climb into the bed, Donna got me to look her in the eye.

"One more, Kathleen. Just one more strong one, and this baby will be here. It will all be over."

At 8:28 am on February 23, 2000, Ryan Alexander joined our family, a healthy eight pounds. I had reached the top of the mountain.

13

Matthew was so thrilled to finally be a big brother! Peggy took him to preschool that morning, and Aaron picked him up at noon and brought him to the hospital. He climbed onto my bed, and I asked him if he would like to meet his new brother. Matthew didn't reply, just held out his arms. The look of satisfaction on his face was priceless: this is my baby. When it was time for us to be discharged from the hospital, Matthew pushed the cart of our things down the hall with such determination, it was as if he was saying, "Out of the way! I'm taking my baby brother home!"

Although we had a few behavior issues in the course of Matthew's adjustment, all his negativity was directed toward me, never toward the baby. Matthew doted upon Ryan, and as he got bigger, Ryan loved nothing more than attention from his big brother. Matthew couldn't wait to show him how each new toy worked, and he loved to try and make Ryan laugh. People kept saying to me, "Just wait until he figures out the baby isn't going away!" But at four years old, Matthew had lots of friends with baby brothers and sisters. He knew that those little people were a permanent part of the family. And now he was part of that special club.

My back felt immediately better once Ryan was delivered, and my recovery went very quickly. I felt so much more myself once my back was not causing me constant pain. A few weeks after Ryan's birth, I resumed physical therapy, and we quickly got my back to stay stable. We worked on strengthening and retraining the muscles to keep the pelvis in place, and after a few months, I was discharged from therapy.

Shortly after Easter, the family gathered to celebrate Ryan's baptism. Our church held baptisms after mass, but to me that made it seem like an afterthought. Welcoming a new member into the community should be a community event, I felt, done as part of a mass. Since St. Thomas would not baptize him during the normal Sunday liturgy, we had a private mass on a Saturday afternoon, and invited all of our friends to attend. The mass was celebrated by a long time friend of my family, Fr. Joe, and members of our folk group provided the music for us. I listened to them sing

"Shepherd Me, O God
Beyond my wants
Beyond my fears
From death into life"

and I marveled at how He had done just that. It had been a long and difficult road, but we had moved from death into life.

Donna said we needed a minimum of two years before we thought about any more babies. My body had been through too much in the past two years, and it needed time to heal. That was fine with me. I was in no rush to start that whole emotionally and physically draining process again soon. Although Aaron and I talked about having more children, the pressure was off since medically I was under orders not to do so yet. I could enjoy just raising my boys.

14

When Ryan turned two, Aaron began to talk more seriously about having another child—after all, we had a green light, right? But I was hesitant. The process of having children thus far had not been an easy one, and I needed to feel really ready to face all the possibilities. After much praying about it, I felt spiritually calm and centered and at peace. It was okay, all that was behind us now. "Go ahead," the voice said. "It will be fine."

In September 2002, we made our annual trip to Camp Trinity. I suspected that I might be pregnant, but my cycles had been going fairly long in recent months, so I was waiting until after the average 35 days before taking a pregnancy test. Aaron was leaving from the retreat for a business trip, however, and I decided I would rather know before he left. So I got up for the Saturday morning prayer service before anyone else was awake, and the test confirmed what my heart already knew.

I went for a walk before the prayer service and enjoyed the peaceful, misty sunrise and time alone with my baby. I planned to share the news with Aaron and my parents later in the day, but I cherished my secret at that moment. It was the only time it would ever be just the two of us. The quiet of the early morning settled into my heart. Ryan's pregnancy had been such a long and stressful experience. It seemed that news of his existence had been given to us at the base of a very tall mountain, with a long journey ahead of us. This time, however, the road felt much flatter. The journey would still take months, of course, but I felt as though it would be a much smoother, more peaceful experience.

A few days later, however, I experienced a day of fear. I was still charting my temperature each day, as I had with Ryan, and it had been lower than usual that morning. I was using the progesterone cream again, and there were no indications of a problem when I went to the bathroom. I tried to tell myself it was just because I got up earlier than usual, but the fear of losing another baby reared up very strong, and there was nothing I could do throughout the day to shake the feeling. I had promised God I would not worry this time, but it seemed that promise might be hard to keep.

We had an ultrasound at seven weeks, just to confirm all was well. The technician was unable to see well enough on the regular abdominal scan and said she would have to do a vaginal scan. My anxiety level shot up instantly. The only time we had ever had to have a vaginal scan was when we lost Victoria, and I prayed we would not have a repeat of that experience. Aaron's tight grip on my hand relaxed, however, with the appearance on the screen of a tiny heart beating right as it should. What a relief! We were given a due date of May 25th—my parents' 35th wedding anniversary.

Although I was feeling queasy, I was thankfully not as sick as I had been with Ryan. Smells bothered me, and Aaron took over the cooking and of washing dishes for most of the next six weeks. The insomnia became a problem again toward the end of the first trimester, but the added hormones from the cream did not seem to cause me nearly as much difficulty as they did with Ryan.

One morning at about 10 weeks, I woke up feeling terrified. I had had a dream that I suddenly began to bleed heavily and lost the baby. I quickly took my temperature, which was up as it should have been, and there were no signs of any bleeding when I went to the bathroom. Everything looked just fine. But the shakiness stayed with me most of the day. I almost called Donna to ask if I could come in for a heartbeat check. I knew she would do it for me, just for peace of mind, but part of me felt foolish calling her about a dream. Stop being an idiot, I told myself. Of course everything is fine. It was only a dream. Finally, I convinced myself I was just being panicky. As the day wore on and there were no signs of trouble, I gradually let go of the dream. But it seemed my promise to remain calm and trusting with this pregnancy was going to be harder than I thought.

At 12 weeks, I went in for a regular prenatal check-up. Everything seemed fine; the weight and measurements were all normal. Then Donna began to listen for the heartbeat. She found the placenta right away, which sounded healthy, but had trouble finding the baby. Even without conversation at this point, I could tell she was beginning be concerned, and my own anxiety level began to climb. Aaron had not been going with me to my monthly appointments, and I was desperately wishing for him to hold my hand. Just when I thought Donna was going to send me across the street to the hospital for an ultrasound, she finally found the heartbeat. The baby was hiding way up in the corner of the womb, but the heartbeat was good and strong. Donna and I shared a look, and each of us exhaled the breaths we had been holding. I think we both had a few gray hairs appear from those tense minutes.

Since we were almost at the end of the first trimester, Donna told me to begin to wean off the progesterone. I think friends and family alike breathed a sigh of relief at that—we were past our personal problem areas. The danger was behind us now, and we could all relax.

Despite the anxiety dream and a few days of fear now and then, I felt I had done a pretty good job of remaining calm. With Ryan's pregnancy, I waited for the other shoe to fall every day. This time I was much more at peace. Now that we were past the first trimester, I just had to hope that my back would remain stable for the rest of the journey.

Even though Ryan was two and a half, he was still sleeping in his crib in the nursery. We were planning to move him in to share a room with Matthew, but since he was not climbing out of his crib, we hadn't been in much of a rush. But now, we decided we should move him sooner rather than later, to put time between his move from the crib and someone else moving into it. So we bought bunk beds for the boys and spent two days following Thanksgiving weekend assembling the beds and rearranging the room. Ryan was thrilled to move to a "big boy" bed and to share a room with Matthew. I had been feeling light butterfly movements from the baby, and the boys couldn't wait for it to be big enough for them to feel it move.

On December 4th, we went in for our 16-week check-up. Aaron and the boys were all along to hear the baby's heartbeat. Donna weighed and measured, and everything was good. Then she began to try and find the heartbeat. "It keeps moving," she said. The time dragged out—it seemed like a half an hour as she searched for the heartbeat, though it was only a few minutes, and my heart began to pound. She kept reassuring us, "I heard it, it's there. But I want you to hear it." Finally, she gave up and said that we needed to do an ultrasound. She set one up at the hospital for a few days later. I was very uneasy.

"Be honest with me," I said. "How worried are you?"

"I'm not really," she answered. "I heard it three times. But since we had a hard time getting a good enough read for you to hear it, I want to be sure everything is okay." It was possible, especially after the previous appointment, that we had a baby who just liked to hide way in the back and the Doppler wasn't picking it up well. But there was also the possibility that the baby was not growing as it should.

Aaron went back to work, and I drove home, fighting back tears all the way. At home, I called my mother at work, something I never do, and she immediately knew there was a problem. I told her about the visit and that Donna didn't seem concerned, but it was hard for me not to worry. She tried to reassure me, as did a friend I called later on. "She's just being careful," they both said. "If she had been really concerned, she would have sent you over to have an ultrasound today. Try to relax." Easier said than done. When Aaron got home, I could no longer hold back the tears. The fear was just so strong.

There was snow the next day, and the kids were off from school. So we made cookies and created art projects for Christmas presents. I tried not to let the nagging fear too near the surface and to focus on enjoying the extra time with the boys. I would take a deep breath and try and blow the anxiety away. But it was like trying to ignore something looking over your shoulder.

By the end of the afternoon, my back was aching—but I'd been on my feet a lot and didn't worry too much. You did too much today, I scolded myself. You should go to bed early tonight.

As I hung up from a phone call around 8:30pm, I started feeling really awful, cold and dizzy. I went to lie down. All of a sudden, I felt a sharp pain in my left side, and my body began to shake. I knew I needed Aaron, but he was downstairs in the playroom with the boys, and even walking a few feet into the hallway was more than I could manage. I went back to bed. I was so cold that even with blankets piled on me I was shivering. I must be really sick, I thought. Matthew came upstairs to get me to see something in the playroom and I told him, "Go get Daddy."

As he left the room, I felt a gush of fluid, and panic set in. By the time Aaron got upstairs, I had made it to the bathroom, but I was bleeding. He called Donna and locked himself in the bathroom with me. She asked him questions about how much bleeding there was, where the pain was—he finally just put me on the phone. I was shaking uncontrollably and bleeding heavily. A particularly strong cramp expelled a large mass of tissue and fluid. Donna had no doubt about what was happening. By 9 pm, it was all over.

Our baby was gone.

15

The boys had been out in the hall this entire time, and they were beginning to get rather hysterical, not knowing what was going on inside the bathroom. I sent Aaron out to be with them and to give them the sad news. Matthew immediately began to cry. Ryan was more confused than anything, but at not quite three, he didn't have much of a way of fully comprehending what was going on. Or so we thought at the time. But Matthew knew what it meant to have a new baby in the house, since he had been four when Ryan was born. He was devastated by the news that the baby had died. By the time I came out of the bathroom, he had drawn me a card that said "I love babies so much," with a picture of a tiny baby with angel wings.

After hugging both of them and trying to offer what comfort I could, I left the task of settling them into bed up to Aaron and went to lie down. My body was still shaking, and I was very cold. Donna had said my body was in shock due to the rapid nature of the delivery. She told me to pile on the blankets so that eventually I would begin to feel warm again. I had asked her if we should go to the hospital. She told me there was nothing they could do and, unless the bleeding seemed excessive, it would be better to be at home in my own bed than in the emergency room. She set a time for us to meet her in the office the next day and told me to try to get some sleep. I knew as well as she that that was unlikely.

It took a while for Aaron to get the boys to sleep—how could they settle down after such a traumatic evening? With the blessing of being children, sleep did come after a while. Aaron was faced with the unenviable task of cleaning up the bathroom. I felt so bad that he had to deal with all of that, but it gave him something to focus on, which I think he needed. Fortunately, the mess was mostly contained in the toilet. After using a slotted spoon to retrieve the baby's body, he came in to the bedroom and asked if I wanted to see the baby. No, I wasn't able to deal with that yet.

Then Aaron then went off to the store for sanitary supplies for me—we had nothing in the house to deal with this level of bleeding. When you deliver a baby in the hospital, the nurses quietly take care of all the cleaning up that goes on for the first few hours. And because you have a beautiful new person to get to know, you don't really focus on what is going on around you. But there was no one to do it for me this time. I had never seen so much blood in my life, and each visit to the bathroom was a reminder that there was no baby to distract me.

While Aaron was at the store, I got up to get some water, and I passed by the hall bathroom. We have a candle holder in the shape of an angel, and Aaron had placed it in the bathroom with the plastic container in which he had placed the baby's body. The candle flickered quietly in the otherwise darkened space. A beautiful little shrine. I stood in the doorway and wiped the tears from my face. My husband, in the midst of trauma, had created a space of peace and reverence. I felt drawn to be with my child, yet I could not bring myself to enter the room again, not after what had just happened.

There was no way I could speak to anyone on the phone, so Aaron was also left with the hard task of calling our parents. My mother knew something was wrong the minute she answered the phone and heard him say, "Ellen, it's Aaron."

"What's wrong?" she asked.

"Our baby died," was all he could say.

The next day was Matthew's seventh birthday, and his party was planned for Saturday afternoon. Was there any way one of my parents could come down and give us some help with the party, Aaron asked my mother. Mom promised they would work it out and told Aaron they would talk to us the following evening.

Aaron's parents, who live in California, were out celebrating his sister's birthday, when he called, so he just left them a message to please give him a call. I suppose they could tell from the tone of his voice that something was very wrong, for they called us back at 2 am our time, something his mother never would have done otherwise. Again, the conversation was very brief—what more could anyone say?

Aaron also called Mary Jo to arrange care for the boys for the next day, since we didn't know how long we would be at Donna's office and whether we would need to go to the hospital. We felt awful that Matthew would be spending his birthday at someone else's house, but it was better not to have the boys with us.

Before he got ready for bed, Aaron took the container from the bathroom and prepared to put it into the refrigerator. I came out into the kitchen as he was doing this, and he asked again if I wanted to see the baby. "Is it scary?" I asked. "No, it's beautiful. Just sad," he replied. He sat at the table, and I stood by his side as he lifted the lid off the plastic tub. There inside was a perfect little human being, eyes closed, as if sleeping on its side. The first thing I remember noticing was the hands, up by the face—five perfect delicate little fingers, the whole hand no bigger than the nail of my pinkie. Long, thin arms and legs, like those of a bird, with tiny little feet with individual toes. Though the baby was so small that it would have fit fully in one of my hands, he or she was perfect. I wanted to touch that tiny little head, but I was afraid I might damage the skin in some way, and I didn't want to risk that. So we just looked at this beautiful little person, held each other, and listened to our hearts breaking.

16

The next morning we took the boys to Mary Jo's house on our way to Donna's office. I stayed in the car while Aaron took the boys inside. I was not ready to see anyone yet.

Donna was watching for us through the side door of the office. She did not want us to have to go through the waiting room of pregnant women. She took us into her office and closed the door. Then she hugged us both, sat down, and and looked at us.

"Did you get any sleep last night?"

"An hour, maybe three," I replied. My voice sounded hollow, even to me.

We had brought the baby with us, and tears came to her eyes as she looked into the container. She was at a loss for words, knowing full well there was nothing she could say to make it any better. She was experiencing just as much disbelief as we were. She looked at both of us with sorrow in her eyes. "I honestly thought things were okay the other day. I never would have let you leave if I had thought we were headed here—we would have gone to ultrasound right then." No one blamed her, of course. There was nothing she could have done, even if we had known. She said she would have Dr. Wolanski look the baby over as well, but as far as she could tell from the initial glance, there did not appear to be anything wrong. I asked if they would be able to tell if it was a boy or a girl—that was very important to me. She said they should be able to, given the gestational age.

She sent us across the street to the hospital for an ultrasound, just to be sure there were no clots or anything that would require surgery. Everything came back clear. When we came back to her office, she said, "It's a boy." Both she and Dr. Wolanski had examined him and he was, as far as they could tell, perfectly healthy. The only thing physical that might have had a problem were the kidneys, and only an autopsy would tell that for sure. No, he was too little—we couldn't stand the thought of that. Donna didn't think that was the problem anyway. She thought a more likely explanation was a viral assault of some kind. Dr. Wolanski could take a tiny tissue sample, she offered, to see if they could get enough cells to grow to be able to detect chromosomal abnormalities. When the chromosomes from both parents line up in the fertilization process, sometimes they do not match up properly or there end up being multiple copies of a gene, which can be incompatible with life. She cautioned that it was iffy whether they would get any information—so many hours had passed since the baby had died that the cells might not grow at all. But it was one way to try and get some answers. We agreed, and Dr. Wolanski took a tiny sample of the baby's skin before we left the office. Donna sent us home, with promises of prayers.

On the way to pick up the children, we stopped at the church to see if we could speak with Fr. Gregory. One of the staff members was shoveling the snow from the sidewalk and saw us get out of the car. It was the middle of the afternoon on a Friday, and we didn't have the children with us—I think he knew immediately that something was wrong.

"Hi, guys. How are you?"

"Not so good," Aaron replied.

"What's wrong?"

"We lost our baby last night."

Frank put down the shovel and enveloped us into a hug. "We are here, whatever you need. This community is here for you." We were still new parishioners, having switched to attending Incarnation that summer, after ten years at St. Thomas. We did not know all that many people in the community, yet Frank's response told me it did not matter. We were not alone.

We asked if Fr. Gregory was in and were told he was away for the day. "But leave him a note. He'll call you as soon as he gets in," Frank promised. We went inside and wrote him a note, explaining what had happened and asking him to call us. Then we went to collect the children.

Mary Jo greeted me with a tearful hug. She made me a sandwich and a cup of tea, since I hadn't eaten much for fear of the possibility of surgery. As we were leaving, she went into her bedroom and came back with a small cross, which she gave us to bury with our tiny son.

On the way home, we told the boys that the baby was a boy, and Matthew was surprised that we knew this. How did we know? We told him that Donna had examined the baby while we were at the office. I guess he had not thought about it, for he asked if we still had the baby. When we told him we did, he asked if he could see him. We were not prepared for that question. We told him we would have to think about it.

We had planned to take Matthew out to lunch for his birthday, but obviously, that had not happened. McDonald's was the rare and favorite treat usually chosen for such occasions, and we promised him we would do so for dinner instead. It was too early to stop for dinner on the way home and I was exhausted, so he agreed to let me rest a while and then we would go back out. But come dinner time, I was still feeling lousy, so I asked him if he would mind if Aaron went and brought it home instead. He began to protest and then stopped and said, "It's okay, Mom. I know you aren't feeling well." We tried to have a happy celebration for him, but I don't think it felt like a birthday celebration to any of us.

We spoke to my parents again that night, and Dad said they would both be coming down the next day. My brother

Mike was coming also. What's more, my parents had cleared their calendars for the next few days and would be staying until Wednesday. I hadn't realized how much I wanted them there until that point. Just knowing there would be someone else there to help take care of the kids and the daily routines made the next few days seem more bearable. Later on, I spoke to my mother about how nice is was for them to have done that, and she told me that after they hung up from Aaron the night before my Dad had wandered around their apartment, trying to find some way to make sense of it all. He wanted to fix it, and there was no way to do that.

"What can I do?" he finally asked my mother.

"There is nothing you can do," she replied.

"No, I can go down there."

They came down on Saturday and helped us get through Matthew's birthday party. I think my parents both thought we were a little crazy to go through with the party, but I felt I had to do it. Everyone would have understood if we had canceled it, but I just couldn't do that to Matthew. It was bad enough that he had lost his little brother—I couldn't take away his birthday, too.

Since my brother did not own a car and would need to be going home before my parents, my parents drove both of their cars down. My father arrived first and helped with the sweeping and setting up while I finished frosting the cake. When he first walked in the door, he didn't say anything, just held me close. No words were necessary to tell me how he felt. I could feel the sorrow and the helplessness in the arms that wrapped around me. When he stepped back, he tried to say something about what had happened. I stopped him with a shake of my head. There would be time for more tears later. I would never get through this day if I began to talk about the baby.

While we were preparing for the party, Fr. Gregory called. He had received our note too late to call us Friday evening. After arranging a time to meet with him on Sunday, he asked how we would be spending the day. I told him we were about to have Matthew's birthday celebration, and he said we could have the celebration for the baby as well, for today he had been born into eternal life. I didn't know how to respond to that, and quickly ended the phone call. Perhaps someday I might be able to look at this from that perspective, but not yet. And right now I needed to try and celebrate this living child.

My mother and Mike arrived shortly before the party began, and Mom took care of all the cleaning up from different activities while Aaron moved the group on to something else. My brother had his grad school final exams in the coming week, and he bravely attempted to study while the chaos of a seven-year-old's birthday party reigned. The kids all had a great time, and when it was over, my father commented on how amazing he thought Aaron and I were. None of the parents whose kids had been there had a clue that anything was wrong. It wasn't that I didn't want people to know what had happened, but I felt it was important to give Matthew an unshadowed party, since his birthday had been so full of sadness. If I had told anyone that day, the wall I had built around myself to allow me to get through the party would have come crashing down.

After Aaron had put the boys in bed, Matthew kept calling for me. When my mother went in to see what he needed, he insisted it had to be me. My mother told him, "Your mother spent a lot of time and energy on your birthday party and she doesn't feel well. She's resting." He was quiet after that, but I got up to go to him anyway. When I kissed him goodnight, I asked him if he had had a good party, and he said, "Oh, yeah, it was exactly what I wanted!" Good, then I had accomplished what I had set out to do.

Now the wall could come down.

17

Aaron and I named the baby Nicholas Sean. He was born on the eve of the feast of St. Nicholas, and St. Nicholas is the patron saint of children. Sean means "God is gracious."

After the boys were asleep, exhausted from the excitement of the party, we asked my family if they would like to see Nicholas. My mother immediately answered yes; my father and brother were unsure. We told them we would not be offended if they chose not to do so, but we would be happy to share him with them, if they wished. In the end, they decided it would be a family viewing. We gathered around the dining room table and Aaron removed the lid from the container. Their reactions to seeing him were the same as I had at first— look at his tiny hands, how perfect. My mother offered up a prayer she remembered from grade school:

> Angel of God, my guardian dear
> To whom God's love commits thee here
> Ever this day be at my side
> To light and guard, to lead and guide.

Though it was very sad to look upon this little body, I think we were all glad we took the opportunity to do so together. Sharing Nicholas with them made me feel like they were mourning him as a person and not just as a hope or a dream. This time, there was not just concern for me, but grief at the death of a grandchild.

We went to church the next day and in the afternoon met

with Fr. Gregory. After greeting us each with a long hug, he opened our time together with prayer. Over the next hour, he asked us questions, listened to us talk, and sat in thoughtful silence; then we planned out how to lay Nicholas to rest. When we asked Fr. Gregory what the procedure was in this kind of case, he said there wasn't one. He had never faced this situation before now, so he didn't have any answers. He would do whatever we wanted—a full funeral mass, or a small service in the cemetery. The full funeral mass didn't seem quite right to either of us, but I will always be grateful for the offer. It recognized my son as fully human. In the end, we settled on a small family service at the cemetery. Fr. Gregory would take care of choosing readings and prayers. All we had to do was tell him when, and he would be there. He ended our session by reading a passage from the book of Lamentations:

> He has filled me with bitterness,
> he has sated me with wormwood.
> He has made my teeth grind on gravel,
> and made me cower in ashes;
> my soul is bereft of peace,
> I have forgotten what happiness is;
> so I say, "Gone is my glory,
> and my expectation from the Lord."
> Remember my affliction and my bitterness,
> the wormwood and the gall!
> My soul continually thinks of it
> and is bowed down within me.
> But this I call to mind and therefore I have hope:
> The steadfast love of the Lord never ceases,
> his mercies never come to an end;
> they are new every morning;
> great is thy faithfulness.
> "The Lord is my portion," says my soul,
> "therefore I will hope in him."
> (Lamentations 3:15-24)

That reading summed up my feelings exactly. As bereft as I felt, I knew God would never abandon me. He was holding all of us in His arms, sheltering us in this storm.

After leaving Fr. Gregory's office, we went looking for a box in which to bury Nicholas. There is a crafter's shop on the pedestrian mall in downtown Charlottesville that carries many forms of art. There we found a small wooden box that almost resembled a cross. It seemed perfect.

Mike had to go home Sunday in order to take his exams, but my parents stayed and took over the running of things for a few days. They drove the kids to school, went grocery shopping, and did the laundry. I think my father had expected me to stay in bed and sleep, so he felt wasn't really resting when I was in the kitchen or on the sofa. But just not having to deal with the normal routine was a rest in and of itself. I have rarely been able to sleep during the day, and I was not able to focus my mind well enough to read. Staying in bed would have meant just staring at the ceiling for hours—I'd rather be doing something.

Aaron had called both of the boy's teachers over the weekend to let them know what was going on. We felt it was very important for them to know before the children went back to school, so they would be prepared for any unusual behavior or questions. They were both very supportive and promised to keep in touch regarding the emotional states of each of the boys. Ryan was being very matter of fact about the whole thing. When our neighbor came over with dinner for us, Ryan said, "Stephen, our baby died." There was no emotion in his voice; he had no real emotional connection to this trauma. But it was better that his teachers were prepared for him to say something than to be taken by surprise. Aside from his birthday party, Matthew had been fairly quiet since Nicholas died. He had not talked much about what had happened and we were not sure if he would say anything to anyone at school or not.

Dad took care of making the arrangements for Nicholas.

Aaron had tried to figure out what we should do after Matthew's party ended, but since it was the weekend we got no answers to our messages at several different locations. Since my parents were there, Aaron went back to work on Monday, knowing he would take more time off later in the week. I opened up the phone book, trying to figure out where to begin. Since we were not having a full funeral mass, we didn't need a funeral home—or did we? I think Dad could tell this was going to be too hard for me, for he offered to make the arrangements. I was so grateful. I stayed with him in the kitchen while he began to make some calls, but after hearing him on the phone describing the situation, I left the room. I just couldn't listen to him explain our loss over and over.

After a while, he came downstairs and said he had talked to one of the funeral homes in town and explained the circumstances. They had recommended a cemetery a mile from our house, where there is an area reserved for infants. Dad called Holly Memorial Garden and found out that there is no charge for the burial or the plot in these cases. The only thing the parents have to pay for is the headstone, if they want one. My father had already told us not to worry about the cost, but this made it easier on everyone. He arranged for Nicholas to be buried on Wednesday morning.

Later that day, I went for an appointment at our family practitioner's office. My body was not dealing well with the massive hormone plummet, and my asthma had flared quite badly. I needed some extra medication to help open up my lungs. The nurse has known us since Matthew was born and could tell that I was feeling awful. She, of course, hadn't heard about Nicholas, so I told her what had happened. She gave me a hug and said she would be sure Dr. Klas knew before he came in to see me. Dr. Klas had been through both of the miscarriages with us and walked the long road of Ryan's pregnancy. He had breathed a sigh of relief just a few weeks earlier when we passed the 12-week danger zone. I knew he would be in shock. He walked in a few minutes later and at first didn't say anything. He enveloped me into a big hug and just stood there a moment.

"Did Susie tell you?" I asked.

"No, Pam did," he replied. "She heard your family prayed for at church this morning and came back and told me. I was planning to call you later, and then I noticed you were on my schedule."

He sat down then. "What happened?"

I told him the story and he said little, resting his head back against the wall and starring at the ceiling in disbelief. As busy as I'm sure his day was, he never acted hurried. There could have been no one else in his schedule that day, for all the time he spent with me. We talked for probably twenty minutes before he even asked what physical problem had brought me in to see him. He checked me out and gave me a prescription, commenting that he wasn't surprised my asthma had gotten bad. Something was going to give under all the stress, and my lungs were so reactive that they are usually the first to flare.

Before Dr. Klas left the room, he asked if he could pray with me. Yes, I would like that. He held my hands and offered up prayers for all the family, for Nicholas, Matthew and Ryan, and for Aaron and me. He prayed for strength for our marriage and support in our grief process. I told him I didn't think he had to worry about the marriage, and he agreed in our case he probably didn't. But, he said, the loss of a child is the most stressful thing a marriage can endure, and many marriages break up over things like this. He wanted to be sure we kept close tabs on each other as we worked our way through this healing process. I assured him we would.

As he was leaving, I said to him, "You know, I now have four babies in Heaven and two on Earth, and those numbers are just wrong."

"You are right," he said, giving me another hug. "They are wrong."

18

Matthew had continued to ask if he could please see his baby brother, and it made Aaron and me quite uneasy. Though there was nothing scary about looking at this perfect little person, was it appropriate for a seven-year-old to see? Aaron's mother, Mary, is a psychiatrist and during one of our phone conversations, I asked her what she thought about Matthew's request. She replied that if he was asking repeatedly and it seemed really important to him, then we should let him view the baby. In the long run, she felt it would help him to work through his feelings of loss. We all agreed, however, that Ryan was too young and should not be present.

Tuesday evening, we told Matthew that we would let him see Nicholas once Daddy got him settled into his wooden box. The box was pretty, but it seemed so hard inside. I couldn't imagine laying a baby down in a wooden crib without something to cushion it and make it cozy, so I took some material and lined the little box. I planned to cover him with some soft material, but somehow using a scrap of fabric just didn't seem right. I had crocheted a blanket for each of my older boys when they were born, I remembered, and I ought to make one for Nicholas, too. But I wasn't sure I could handle making it, even though it would be only a few inches wide and would take me all of ten minutes to do. Emotionally, it was hard to think about making it. But, in the end, I decided I needed to do this.

My father sat across the kitchen table from me, watching me struggle not to cry while crocheting this little square. He reached over and put his hand over mine and said, "You don't have to do this." Though I couldn't express it to him at the time, I knew that I had to do this. It was the only chance I would have to be a mother to my child. And somehow, even though I knew he would never know the difference, knowing Nicholas would be tucked in cozy and warm made it slightly easier to say goodbye.

Thankfully, Ryan fell asleep early that evening. After Aaron got Nicholas transferred to the box, we took Matthew into the kitchen so he could see him. My parents sat on one side of the table, and Matthew sat on Aaron's lap. We took off the lid and watched Matthew's face. He didn't cry, but said "Oh" the way people do when they see a new kitten. He looked at Nicholas' hands and feet, commenting on how tiny he was. After a few minutes, I let him help me cover Nicholas with the tiny blanket and lay Mary Jo's cross on top of him. I asked Matthew if there was anything he would like to put in the box with Nicholas, and he said yes and went to his room. He came back with two polished stones from his collection and placed them very tenderly at the feet of his brother, blinking back tears.

The Charlie Brown Christmas special was on TV that night, and when the clock struck eight, Matthew lifted his head, knowing the show was about to start. He did not seem to know what to do—he did not want to miss the show, but he did not want to leave either. I asked him if he was ready to say goodbye to Nicholas and go watch Charlie Brown, and he nodded. With one last look, he said, "Goodbye, Nicholas" and fled. My mother followed him downstairs, leaving me and Aaron with my father in the kitchen. I think it was a good thing that the timing of the viewing had been so close to the start of the show. Matthew had a distraction to put some distance between seeing Nicholas and having to go to sleep, and by the time the show was over, he was ready for bed. Children often need to process difficult life moments in small pieces—I think the time he spent with Nicholas was as much as he could handle right then.

Aaron and I sat for a few more minutes with our tiny son, both of us reluctant to take the final step of sealing the box. It went against everything we expected to do as Nicholas' parents. Parents cuddle and rock their babies; they don't shut them in a box. Finally, with a squeeze of my hand, Aaron picked up the lid and closed the box, and my heart, which I didn't think could hurt any more, broke again.

19

Wednesday was cold and icy, nasty weather to be out. Freezing rain had made the roads very slick. Schools were closed, and we were not sure we would be able to have the ceremony that morning—the frozen ground might prevent digging the grave. But a call to the cemetery at 10 am confirmed that they would be able to open the ground. We would go ahead as scheduled. An hour later, we met Fr. Gregory and Deacon Chris at the cemetery.

As if the day were not going to be difficult enough, things did not go smoothly once we got there. My father had picked up all the required paperwork from the cemetery office on Monday, and we had filled it out at home. Dad had dropped it off on Tuesday, confirming when he did so that everything was in order for the burial on Wednesday. But when we arrived, the man in the office could not find our paperwork anywhere—after searching for it for almost ten minutes, he told us we would have to fill it out again.

While I began that tedious process, the cemetery workers began to discuss the lack of a steel box into which to place Nicholas' wooden box. Virginia law required it, for environmental reasons, but it usually comes from the funeral home. Since we had not used a funeral home, there was a question as to whether they should charge us for the box. In addition, we had no death certificate, which the cemetery was required to have on file before burial. The office manager was back and forth with his supervisor on the phone, coming in to ask us questions, going back to the phone to discuss the responses. Finally, he asked me to speak to his supervisor directly.

Why didn't this baby have a death certificate? I had to explain that because Nicholas was less than twenty weeks gestation, his death was classified as a miscarriage by the state, and there is no death certificate for miscarriages. We would receive a "certificate of fetal demise" from the state, but it would probably be several weeks before we received that. Why had I not been in the hospital? This question required a description of the rapid nature of Nicholas' delivery and the lack of time to get to the hospital. Why had the funeral home not given us the steel box? I replied that since we were having a private burial service without a funeral mass beforehand, the funeral home had told us we did not need to go through them for his burial. No one had said anything in the previous three days of making the arrangements about needing state paperwork or steel boxes.

As this conversation continued, I was getting increasingly annoyed. Describing to a stranger over the phone why I had not been in a hospital when my baby died was not what I needed to be doing on the morning of my baby's funeral! I felt I was having to defend my right to be there at all. The unspoken question from this supervisor was why we were burying the product of a miscarriage. It was clear to me that both the man in the office and his supervisor thought this whole burial should be called into question.

All this time, Fr. Gregory and Deacon Chris were waiting in the hall, talking with my parents. We were running against a clock, as they had to be back at the church in time for the 12:15 daily mass. I turned the phone back over to the office manager and sat back down at the table with the paperwork. Aaron had been outside the office during the phone conversation, but he had observed enough of the conversation to know what an ordeal it had been for me. He squatted next to my chair and and pulled my head to his shoulder. This day was hard enough on both of us—the lack of professionalism from those in the office was rubbing on nerves that were already raw.

Finally, the supervisor decided they should give us the steel box. The smallest one they had was usually used for infants, but was meant for caskets of full term infants. So when we placed a six inch wooden box into it, it looked lost. The manager looked very confused at the size of the box, but he made no comment, thankfully. A workman secured the top on the box and carried it outside. Because I had spent ten minutes on the phone with the supervisor, the paperwork was still not completed, but we convinced the man to let us go ahead with the service and to finish the paperwork afterwards.

They led us out to where the canopy was set up and though the freezing rain had stopped, it was very cold and raw. But sunshine would have felt wrong. Fr. Gregory gave a brief reading and prayer and then gave each of us the opportunity to say goodbye to Nicholas by touching his box. Ryan was squirming around, not seeming to pay too much attention, but he did go over and touch the box at Fr. Gregory's invitation. As soon as the final prayer was said, Fr. Gregory and Deacon Chris had to leave, to get back in time for mass. I hugged them each goodbye and turned back toward the grave site. There was Aaron, with tears streaming down his face.

In general, men do not let their emotions show as readily as women, and Aaron was no exception. Perhaps he had felt the need to be strong and supportive for me, whose body had been through such trauma, or perhaps he just did not know how to let his emotions out. I had been able to read the grief in his eyes and his body language, but tears had been kept private, if they had fallen.

Now, as I held my sobbing husband and shared his tears, I noticed Matthew sitting on the platform next to Nicholas' box, staring off into space. Aaron and I went over to him while my parents quietly got Ryan out of the way and went back inside. I knelt down beside my oldest child and put my arms around him. He wasn't crying, just starring off into space.

"You know," I said, "it's okay to feel really sad. It's okay to cry."

"I know."

But there were no tears, just silence. I told him we were all feeling bad and would for a while, and we would have to be gentle with each other, too. I tried to explain to him how Ryan didn't really understand because he was so young. He probably would not remember this the way Matthew would, either, and that was not his fault.

"Just the way you don't remember when we lost our other babies in Heaven."

He turned to look at me. "What other babies in Heaven?"

"You see, that is my point. We have three other babies in Heaven with Nicholas. One died before you were born, and you were only Ryan's age when we lost the other two. And you don't remember, do you?"

He shook his head and was silent a moment.

"Are they buried somewhere, too?" he asked softly.

"No, sweetie, they were too little."

We sat with him in silence while he processed all this new information. After a while, we asked him if he was ready to go.

"No."

"Okay, we'll stay until you are ready." My arm was still around his shoulders as he continued to stare off into space.

"Mom, I can't leave him here."

There were still no tears from Matthew, but Aaron and I both struggled to maintain our own composure. Our seven-year-old was wrestling with strong grown-up emotions. Matthew had voiced what each of us were feeling. No parent should have to bury their child, and no child his sibling.

Leaving Nicholas in a box in the ground went against everything we knew as right. There was nothing we could say to him other than, "We have to, Matthew."

After a while of sitting in silence, he let us take him inside to warm up while we finished up the paperwork and chose the headstone. I didn't know it until much later, but my mother had had a long conversation with the guy from the office while we had been outside. He evidently was still confused as to why we were burying this tiny box and began to ask my mother questions about Nicholas. Had she seen it? Yes, she had. Did it look human? Yes, *he* did. My mother sat and described to this man Nicholas' tiny individual fingers and perfect little feet. A human baby, just a very small one. He sat quietly for a while, then said, "If you look like a human being, you should be buried like a human being."

It's probably a very good thing I was not there to witness this conversation, for who knows what I might have said. When my mother told me about this later, my reaction was, why did he think we were there, for goodness sake? But Mom took a different view. Perhaps this man learned something today and would treat another family faced with this horrible experience with a different respect. If so, then Nicholas' short life had already impacted someone else on this earth.

20

How hard it was to drive away from the cemetery that morning—even more so when Matthew repeated, "Mom, I can't leave him here." We promised we would be back to visit Nicholas, and he wanted to know when. The headstone would not be ready for several weeks, and we told him we would wait until it was put in so we would know exactly where he was. But that seemed like a long time to Matthew. I, on the other hand, wasn't sure I'd ever be able to go back and visit. We live only a mile or so from the cemetery, and driving by it every day was going to be hard enough. My father had thought that being close by would be a comfort in the long run, which has become true, over time. But in those first few months, my heart broke every time we passed by, several times a day.

My parents left after we had lunch, and we were on our own for the first time since Nicholas had died. We tried to figure out how to resume normal life—what was normal at this point? Our annual Christmas party was scheduled for the coming weekend, and my mother had been urging us to cancel it. But Advent, the time of preparation for Christmas, has always been one of my favorite times of year, and I needed to try and find something of the usual Advent joy. If we had canceled it, what would we have done with ourselves that night but sit around and feel even more lost? Besides, all the guests are good friends, and they all knew what had happened. Mary Jo and Peggy offered to come early and help with preparations, and we just didn't worry too much about cleaning. The party was a bit more subdued than usual, but having the support of good friends and a distraction for a while proved to be a good decision.

However, finding the joy of Advent proved to be impossible. We went to an Advent concert at church, filled with beautiful readings and music about the coming of our Savior, and I felt so empty inside. Towards the end of the concert, the choir sang a song I had never heard, whose first verse had me in tears:

> A time will come for singing
> When all your tears are shed
> When sorrow's chains are broken
> And broken hearts shall mend.

It seemed almost that God was speaking directly to me in that song, but right then it was hard to believe there would ever be a time when my heart would mend and my tears would be done flowing.

After the concert, Deacon Chris told us how glad he was to see us there. I told him I was having a very hard time finding Advent this year, and he just shook his head.

"Then don't try," was all he said.

Aaron came down with a cold, which I promptly caught as well. Since my lungs were already struggling, the cold quickly settled into my chest and became bronchitis. Another trip to the doctor had me on antibiotics and decongestant, so everyone would be well in time for Christmas. It didn't feel like Christmastime. I not only felt robbed of my child but of my favorite time of the year as well. But as disconnected from the season as we felt, we still had two other children to think about, and they deserved to have as happy a Christmas as we could manage. I continued to do the preparations, baking and decorating, but my body was battered and my heart felt empty.

At the school's winter music program in the middle of December, one of the mothers I had known since Matthew's preschool days came up and gave me a hug, the kind that told me she knew about Nicholas. When I asked her how she knew, she said, "Rachel told me. She got in the car the other day and told me she had some sad news. Matthew's little brother had gone to sleep in his mom's tummy and died." Matthew had shared the exciting news of the pregnancy with his first-grade class when we had told him earlier in the year. When we checked with his teacher after the music program, she confirmed that Matthew had shared the news of his brother's death with the class at circle time earlier that week. Other than that and seeming to need a little more physical closeness, such as sitting on her lap, however, she assured us it didn't seem to be adversely affecting his days at school.

On Christmas Eve, my family returned. I had made a vest for Ryan to wear on Christmas Eve and was desperately trying to finish the one for Matthew before it was needed for church that night. My sewing machine was not cooperating, and I finally fell to sewing it by hand. My mother urged me to let it go. Matthew could wear something else. Why was I pushing myself on this, especially when I wasn't feeling well? I finally found a way to express it—nothing else had gone right this month. This project was the one thing over which I felt I had any control right now, and I needed to have at least one thing successfully completed. I don't think she understood, but she left it alone, and I did manage to get the vest at least in a wearable state. To this day, it does not have button holes, but Matthew was very proud of it, nonetheless.

As we decorated the house for Christmas and put the stockings on their hooks, Matthew noticed that there was not a stocking for Nicholas. I had made stockings for both Matthew and Ryan for their first Christmas, and Matthew felt that I should make one for Nicholas. He envisioned a full-size stocking like his and Ryan's, but that did not seem appropriate to me or to Aaron. And it was something I was just not able to do emotionally. So Matthew decided he would make a stocking for Nicholas. We cut out a small stocking from some blue furry material, and he sewed it together on his own, with just a small amount of help with the hard parts. I wrote Nicholas' name on it with fabric paint, and suggested we would hang it on the Christmas tree as an ornament. But Matthew wanted to hang it with his and Ryan's. I gently reminded him that Santa wasn't going to fill Nicholas' stocking, and he wondered why not. "Because Nicholas isn't here." I told him. He didn't like the idea of it hanging empty, so on Christmas Eve, he filled it with some of his special stones and marbles so that there would be something in the stocking for Nicholas on Christmas morning. It was a very sweet gesture, though it made my heart ache to look at it. As hard as it was for me to see it hanging there, I did not say anything. It was important to Matthew that his brother be included in the family Christmas traditions, and we needed to support his feelings and his healing as much as our own.

Christmas Eve service proved to be much more difficult for me than I had anticipated. It felt almost like being in a bubble, looking at a foreign world but not being really present. All around me, people were singing, full of joy at remembering the birth of Jesus. This wonderful time of year, filled with happiness and light, to me seemed dark and hollow. And those in the pews around us had no idea that we did not share in their joy. I wasn't able to sing because of my respiratory infection, and I couldn't have gotten through any of the songs anyway. After all, what are all the Christmas songs about? "For unto us a child is born!" "Unto us a son is given!" Except my son had been taken away.

By the middle of the day on Christmas Day, the coughing from the bronchitis was turning into wheezing, something I never do, not even in the midst of an asthma attack. A visit to the doctor's office the day after Christmas confirmed that despite the antibiotics, the infection had gone deeper into my chest. It wasn't full-blown pneumonia, but only because I was already on antibiotics.

While my family was there, my mother kept asking what she could do to help with things around the house. I had not been in the nursery since Ryan had moved out of it—even the sheets were still on the crib. Our bedroom door faces that of the nursery, and I could not stand to look at the room each time I went in our out of our bedroom. I begged Aaron to take the crib down. There was no way I could see that empty nursery for months on end, knowing there would be no baby to come home to it. So Aaron and my father disassembled the crib and packed it away, and Mom packed up all the sheets and baby linens so I wouldn't have to do it. She also emptied my closet of the maternity clothes I no longer needed.

21

We got through the rest of the holidays, and as January began, we tried to begin to resume life. My body took a while to heal, but it was far faster than my heart. I felt empty, sad, and angry. I wanted to stamp my foot like a child and scream, "It's not fair!" Because it wasn't fair. Hadn't we already been through enough?

We still had no explanation for what had happened. The tissue sample Dr. Wolanski took from Nicholas did not grow healthy cells, so the lab technicians were unable to map Nicholas' chromosomes. There was no way to know if there had been a genetic problem. Then Sharon gave us what became the most likely answer.

Three weeks before Nicholas died, I had met her and Mary Jo for tea on a Friday morning. During the early hours of Sunday morning, all three of us had gotten sick, within an hour or so of each other. We figured we had picked up some weird stomach virus at the coffee shop. And yet, no one else in any of the three households came down with it. All the doctors we spoke to about it in the following weeks had agreed—it had to be food borne. If it were that strong a stomach virus that all three of us had gotten it, at least one of the seven other people in the three households would have gotten sick. Sharon pointed to that as a possible reason. Look at all the literature about listeriosis and other food-borne illnesses that they warn pregnant women about, she said.

Pregnant women are told to avoid eating soft cheeses, such as brie, or drink any unpasteurized juices because of the risks of bacteria. Infections of listeriosis are relatively rare, but cause fever, vomiting, and diarrhea—and can lead to miscarriage and stillbirth if untreated in pregnant women. The symptoms and timing were all there.

With an otherwise seemingly healthy baby, Donna had been looking at a viral attack as the most probable cause of Nicholas' death. When we mentioned Sharon's theory to her, she agreed that that was the most likely explanation. I had called her at the time I became sick to see if there was anything to be concerned about, but it had seemed to both of us that it was some kind of a stomach virus; and as long as I did not spike a dangerously high fever or get too dehydrated, there was no risk to the baby. There was no reason for anyone to suspect a food-borne illness at the time—it was only through our husbands talking at church about the fact that all the wives were sick that we even made the connection to the Friday morning tea date. There was no way to go back and test for the disease, but all the pieces did create a complete picture. Donna was 99 percent sure we had our answer. Tragic and senseless, and totally unfair. We had had a car accident when I was almost eight months along with Matthew, and he had been fine—I had a cup of tea and a scone, and my child died. Which of those should have been a major life-altering event?

I felt like the rug had suddenly been pulled out from under my feet, and underneath was an ice rink. My whole world had been turned upside down in an instant. I wasn't angry at Donna—there was nothing she could have done, and she grieved right along with us. I wasn't really angry at God, either. I never felt as if He had deliberately taken my child away. But I felt betrayed.

Why didn't you stop it? I asked Him. Why didn't you protect Nicholas? I voiced that thought to a friend of mine a few weeks after the holidays were over. Why didn't God protect him? I wondered.

"Maybe He did," she said. "Maybe by not interfering, God protected you and Nicholas from something much worse that you couldn't have handled. If that illness made the adults so sick, who knows what it might have done to a developing baby. We don't know what might have been—only God can see that. So perhaps He did protect him."

Her response temporarily defused the anger. Perhaps God chose the better outcome, as hard as it was. I could live with that. But the feelings of betrayal remained. Did God know when we conceived Nicholas that he would die on that day? If so, why did He allow those events to take place that led to this outcome?

I never felt distanced from God—He was always right there. But I felt like I was sitting on the sofa next to a close friend who had hurt me. You told me it would be okay this time! You let me feel at peace about this pregnancy. How could you let this happen?

Despite how awful I felt inside, I did recognize that we were very fortunate to have an amazing support system. Both of our families kept in close contact and helped us work through those first few months. Friends emailed and called. We felt the prayers of so many people, surrounding us and holding us up.

As we got into the new year, life began to go on—for everyone but me. People expect after a few weeks that you should be getting yourself together by now—after all, it's been a month. But I wanted to shout "It's ONLY been a month!" Everywhere I looked, it seemed there were pregnant women. Everywhere I turned, there were reminders of what should be. Except this time, I didn't force myself to go places that were hard and try to be strong. I avoided what I could avoid to spare myself any extra pain. Aaron began taking Matthew to his music class each week, because I couldn't bear to sit across from the mother of a classmate who was also due in May. I tried to sit away from babies in church and avoided talking to pregnant women as much as I could.

I wanted to curl up in someone's lap like a hurting child and have my tears kissed away. To have someone hold and soothe me and magically make my pain go away. I wanted to run away and be alone. I longed to walk the beach and try and find solace in voice of the waves. To distance myself from all my obligations and focus on trying to repair my spirit, which felt flattened and torn to shreds. If my parent's beach apartment had not been undergoing renovations and been uninhabitable, I would have gone off by myself for a few days. But as that was not an option, I struggled on with day to day life.

There were many days when all I wanted to do was pull the covers over my head and hide from the world. My heart was broken—why should I pay attention to the rest of the world? But I couldn't do that. I had two little boys who needed their mother. I had to get up and get them ready for school each day, make lunches, drive the carpool, and do the laundry. There is no question that having the other children to take care of forced me to get back to "normal life" as soon as the holidays were over. But everyday tasks seemed to take much more effort. The laundry was a burden, not just a household chore. I didn't have the energy for cleaning the bathrooms or vacuuming the playroom. And my emotional state was so rocky that I didn't have much patience with my children, which bothered me more than anything. I tried hard to keep life on an even keel for them, but I know there were many times when I snapped at them for reasons for which they were not to blame.

In mid-January, I went up to a meeting at the theater and stepped in to watch a few minutes of rehearsals for Once Upon a Mattress. We had not auditioned in December, for obvious reasons. A friend of ours, who was stage managing the production, came over to stand beside me.

"This looks like it is going to be a fun one," I said, watching the cast learn a dance sequence.

"You want in?"

He offered to talk to the director. It might be good for you guys right now, he said. He went over and had a word with the director, then came back and said, "You want in, you've got a spot. Both of you. Go home and talk to Aaron."

Perhaps he was right. We thought about it, and although there was concern among our family and friends about me having the physical strength for rehearsals and performances, we decided it was a good thing to do. We had many good friends up at Four County Players now, and perhaps just being in their company would aid in the healing process. Once again, the theater became a refuge. Rehearsals were a welcome distraction, and the show gave us a reason to laugh.

I was definitely better off when I was around other people. The sadness didn't go away, but when I was alone it seemed to grow to the point of engulfing me. Days that I stayed at home after taking the boys to school were particularly bad. Despair seemed to creep in on me when I was alone, like I was at the bottom of a well and the world was collapsing in on me. But as in the poem "Footprints," it was at those lowest and saddest points that I felt the hand of God holding me. One day while I was trying to do the laundry, I just sat down on the basement steps, put my head into my arms, and sobbed. I missed my baby so much that my chest physically hurt. My heart felt empty and crushed, my spirit flattened. As I sat there, I sensed a presence next to me on the step, and an arm come around my shoulder. Like a mother comforting a child at her breast, the angel just held me and let me cry. I can't say that I magically felt healed and whole, but even in those darkest of days, I felt I was never totally alone.

Being around other people made it easier to seem strong. No one likes to fall apart in front of others, and I think most people looked at me and thought, "She's so strong, she's handling this so well" or "She's moved on." Close friends knew I was struggling, for they could read it on my face—or get a straight answer when they asked how I was doing.

Perhaps I should have let more people know how I was really doing, but society doesn't know how to deal with people who are grieving, and the emotions that surface during grief make people uncomfortable. So to the outside world, I put on a mask of coping.

One day, a friend of ours at the theater was surprised to hear me make a comment about the grief and asked, "Are you still dealing with that?" He thought both Aaron and I seemed much better than when we had first begun rehearsals for the show. I just told him, "You don't see me at home" and let it at that. The makeup table a few minutes before the curtain rose was not the place to make a scene. But inside I was raging: Am I still dealing with it? If one of my older boys had died, would anyone say that to me, expect me to be fine three months later? I hadn't even gotten to my due date yet! I was trapped in a pregnancy that didn't exist.

22

I dreaded Nicholas' due date—it loomed like a big black cloud on the horizon. Well-meaning friends said, "Maybe you'll be pregnant again by then." No, that I will not. Getting pregnant with another child needs to be a joyful thing, because we want to bring another child into our family, not as a means of trying to forget this one. Another baby would never replace Nicholas, nor should one be conceived to try and do so. And I needed to finish Nicholas' pregnancy before I could even think of another.

I had no idea how I would ever find the courage to face another pregnancy. I told Fr. Gregory that a lot of trust would have to be built up before that could happen, and how do you rebuild the trust when you feel as if it is God that has betrayed you? I wasn't even able to figure out which way to turn to try and find that path. He told me to stand still and not to turn. I told him I didn't even know how to pray about any of this, and he told me all I had to say was, "Lord, I'm lost. Please find me." As I thought about that, I realized that that is exactly what we tell a child when we go to places away from home—if you ever become separated from me, stay there, don't move, and I will find you.

People began to ask if we were going to "try again;" a phrase I came to hate. To me, it took away the sense that Nicholas was a person, and it implied that I failed at something. After all, as the saying goes, "If at first you don't succeed, try, try again." But I hadn't failed at something, my child died. Except I had failed at something—I had failed to protect him. I knew it wasn't good for me to blame myself, and I didn't really, even though it seemed that something I had eaten had taken his life. There was no way to know that a cup of tea and a scone could have such dire consequences. People commented upon how I had nurtured him in his short little life, and yet I still felt that I had failed to protect him. Donna told me that given how much sicker my friends were than I that day, my immune system had been in overdrive and had done everything in its power to protect that baby. And yet I couldn't shake the feeling that it hadn't been enough.

If we had made the connection to the illness being food-borne right away instead of weeks later, might we have been able to treat it and save him? If I had started antibiotics quickly enough, could we have protected him from the infection? Donna had no answer to my questions. Antibiotics, begun quickly after diagnosis, can prevent the bacteria from infecting the baby, but that is most often in the third trimester, when most of the development of the baby's organ systems is complete. Nicholas was still so small, still developing his internal organs, that even if we had known right away, it might not have been enough to save him. And, she gently reminded me, we should not blame ourselves for information we did not have.

At the beginning of February, we received the certificate of fetal demise in the mail. It wasn't even a certificate, but a photocopy of the "report of spontaneous fetal death" that Donna had submitted to the Virginia Department of Health in Richmond. Reading it, anger welled up inside me—the state did not consider him human enough to warrant a death certificate. When do you magically become a human being, I wondered. Where is the line that you must cross? After twenty weeks gestation, a woman is required to go through labor to deliver a fetus that has died; a D&C is no longer an option because the death is considered a still birth. Are you considered human at twenty weeks gestation but not at nineteen and a half weeks? If Nicholas had lived four weeks longer, he would have been about ten inches long instead of six, and he would have weighed almost a pound instead of seven or eight ounces. The only difference would have been his size. Does being bigger make you more human?

Before twenty weeks gestation, the medical field considers a pregnancy loss to be a miscarriage. But it is not a miscarriage when you bury a child, I had told Donna in our most recent conversation. I had delivered an extremely premature stillborn baby.

"Yes," she agreed. "You did. And because the state considers it to be a miscarriage is all the more reason to be thankful you were at home when it happened."

"What?!" I said, remembering the trauma to the boys, the mess Aaron had to deal with alone.

"No one could dispute your right to bury that baby," she replied.

"Wait a minute," I said. "Are you telling me that if Nicholas had been born in the hospital, we would not have had the right to take him home to bury him?"

"That is correct."

"You are kidding me." I still could not believe what she was saying.

"Nope. Dr. Wolanski has had to argue this issue with the hospital on behalf of his patients several times, and the result was usually only the ashes of the baby, not the body." She paused. "As hard as it was for you and Aaron to deal with that night by yourselves, it was better for everyone concerned that you were at home."

Now, as I looked at the "report of spontaneous fetal death," it seemed so clinical. It recorded how many years of education I had, whether or not I had smoked or taken drugs during the pregnancy, how many other pregnancies I had had, the suspected cause of fetal death, and even how much weight I had gained thus far in the pregnancy—but no where did it ask the baby's gender. The line that Donna had to sign "certif[ied] that this delivery occurred and the fetus was born dead." So the state considers a developing baby to be alive, but not human enough to even ask its gender? The only place where there would be a record of Nicholas Sean Olowin ever having existed would be the cemetery. When, I wondered again, does a person become a person?

23

In March, at the urging of my mother and several friends, I began working with a therapist. When I called to set up an appointment, I told her I had been referred to her for post-partum depression, a form of depression that sometimes affects women after the birth of a child. It was, at least in my view, the best explanation for why I was making the appointment. At the end of our first session, however, she told me: "I'm not looking at a depressed person. I'm looking at a grieving mother, and there is a big difference."

I had been getting the feeling that other people were beginning to think I was "dwelling" on this too much, still talking about Nicholas and having a cloud of sadness around me. I had never dealt with feelings of sadness for such an extended period of time before this—even the other losses we had experienced did not compare. Perhaps it was a cumulative thing. I had no energy, no desire to do anything. Housework was a burden, chores went undone. But I had children who needed me, obligations to fulfill. The rest of the world saw me getting on with life, but slowly. The therapist validated the fact that grief is a long, personal process and that no one should expect a mother to be done grieving for her child, even a child she had never met, in a matter of weeks or even months. She understood my feeling of still being trapped in the pregnancy and felt that I would be doing much better once we got past his due date. I prayed she was right.

May was a tough month as we approached the time when Nicholas should have been born. The weather was beautiful —spring in Virginia is such a wonderful time. But the beauty of the azaleas and dogwoods only made me more aware of how dark my world seemed. The colors all had a film over them, like I was viewing them through a tinted window. The month went by so slowly. As we approached his due date, my arms ached to hold him, and my heart felt full of tears. I hated the way I looked when I looked in the mirror—I shouldn't be my normal shape, I should be very round. The desire to get pregnant again was very strong that month, though I knew I was not emotionally ready for it. Even if I had wanted to act upon that urge, I was on too many spring allergy/asthma medications to do so safely. And the last thing we wanted was to add any unnecessary risk factors. It was probably a good thing that medically I was restricted from acting upon those urges, for I didn't want to try and replace Nicholas, and right then, that's what I would have been doing.

The last few days leading up to his due date were very hard. I had anticipated that the weekend would be tough, and I could feel it building up all week long. Thankfully, God gave us a buffer zone of distractions that weekend. My parents and my brother came down, and the adults all went to dinner and a play Saturday night to celebrate Aaron's and my mother's birthdays and my parents 35th wedding anniversary. Two sets of out-of-town friends called Saturday afternoon to say they were in town unexpectedly, and we invited them all over for a cookout on Sunday.

We had arranged for the morning mass on the 25th to be said in Nicholas' memory. When we had decided not to have a full funeral mass at the time of his burial, we had agreed we would have a mass said for him at a later date. His due date seemed the appropriate time. Sitting in church that morning, I became aware that the readings, the songs, and the sermon all reflected the theme of the love of God. I felt surrounded by it all through mass, as if a comforting voice were saying, "Yes, this day is difficult. But I am here."

My parents and my brother went with us to the cemetery after mass. The visit to his grave was difficult, but necessary. It was the only physical connection I could have with Nicholas that day, and I needed to be near him. Though I knew he would never know if we had been there or not, somehow, to not have gone and visit his grave would have felt uncaring. The boys decorated the stone with buttercups and rocks, and I tried hard to keep from crying. I was afraid I would be unable to stop if I allowed the tears to begin, so I swallowed them. I wanted so much to hold him—the cold gravestone only made the pain in my chest that much stronger. My heart ached for Nicholas—I should be visiting him in the nursery, not the cemetery!

After my family went home, our friends came over to our house for the cookout. I think only a few of them realized what day it was or what a great service they were providing by being there and distracting us from the day, but it was obvious to me that God knew we needed them all so much. The visit to the cemetery had been emotionally draining, and the rest of the day would have been very long without our friends there. The sun was shining in a bright blue sky, and we spent the whole afternoon outside in the back yard. The children played tag and baseball, coming back to the table for bites of hamburger and chips in between innings. The adults talked and caught up on what the kids were doing in school, what was happening for each of the dads at work. The afternoon slipped away in the comfort of family fun. I think God knew I couldn't handle focusing on Nicholas all day.

After our guests left, the four of us went as a family to the garden supply store and chose a tree for Nicholas—a living memorial to him. Together we decided on a weeping cherry, a tree with beautiful, delicate flowers and a tearful name. We planted it in our front yard on Memorial Day, and at last the pregnancy came to a close.

24

Shortly after Nicholas' due date, baby things began arriving in the mail: formula samples, diaper coupons, new mom magazines. I began to dread going to the mailbox each day, for fear of what other reminders I might find waiting for me. I would tear up the coupons with vehemence, as if taking out some of my anger on the paper would take the sting out of receiving them day after day. How did I get on their mailing lists? And how do I get off?

If being around pregnant women had been difficult in the past few months, being around newborns now was even more so. The pregnancy was over, but my arms were aching to hold the baby who wasn't there. On the weekend in June that baptisms were held at our church, I made sure we were out of town. I could not handle being there watching other babies be baptized on the day Nicholas should have been.

However, even now, another pregnancy was far from my mind. If I had just given birth, would I want to jump right into another pregnancy? Emotionally, this pregnancy just ended. I still needed time to heal. We decided to make no decisions about another baby for a while. To just be, for a while. For how many times could we put these broken hearts back together?

Getting into June didn't magically make everything right again, and I hadn't expected it to do so. Yet, as the summer went by and the boys and I traveled and played, the good days began to outnumber the bad, and the pain in my heart dulled to an ache. I wanted to get back to normal, but I knew from our past experiences that we could never go back to the way things were before Nicholas died. Our lives had been forever changed and we were not the same people we were before losing him. We were now a different road than we had been, and normal meant learning to recognize this new path as ours. As the days went by, I began to see more of the good things in the life going on around me. There were still things that were hard—being around babies didn't get any easier to be sure—but life was slowly finding a new sense of normal.

My days were brighter, and my emotions more stable, but I still struggled with an overwhelming sense of fear. After losing Joshua and Victoria I arrived at a place where I felt I was stronger as a person as a result of those experiences. This time, I continued to wrestle with the conflicting feelings of wanting to have another baby and being terrified of the prospect of doing so. I honestly didn't think it would ever go away this time—and how can you face a pregnancy with that much anxiety?

Toward the end of the summer, I began to have some gynecological soreness issues that Donna had trouble solving. They definitely seemed to be hormonal in nature, occurring on the same days of each menstrual cycle. I had been through something similar before becoming pregnant with Ryan, after having the two miscarriages in an row. Perhaps there was something about the sudden hormone plummet that threw things out of balance. Something was definitely out of whack with the cycle of hormones, even though my cycles remained as usual. Donna felt that it was something I was going to have to deal with as part of my sensitive skin, but I felt there was a connection to Nicholas' death.

Either way, we needed to find a way to soothe the very tender skin. Had I recently switched to a new soap, new laundry detergent, anything like that? I hadn't, and irritation from a product would probably be continual, not cyclical. But

Donna decided I should avoid using anything but water in washing and that Aaron and I should switch to using Natural Family Planning as our birth control method for a while. Natural Family Planning uses the woman's basal body temperatures and physical changes in vaginal secretions as markers for the onset of ovulation, and that meant being extra careful, since getting pregnant had never been one of our difficulties. Because my menstrual cycles still fluctuated in length, Donna gave us narrow "safe zones" at the beginning and end of each month.

There were still so many fears churning inside I couldn't imagine facing a pregnancy yet, so I was very careful to keep track of my charts. Months that the cycle went longer, I would find myself worrying that I might be pregnant, being relieved at the start of the cycle, and that was not the attitude I wanted to take. Pregnancy should not be looked at as something to fear. But I was petrified at the thought of losing another baby. I truly did not believe I could survive it again. How far could I bend before I broke completely? We wanted to have another child, and I didn't want our last experience with pregnancy to be one of death. But making a conscious decision to get pregnant again was something I didn't think I would ever be able to do. How was I going to find the courage to face that long road again? Perhaps the only way was not to make a conscious decision, but to place it in God's hands. As winter approached, I tried to relax and let go of the anxiety. If we were meant to have another child soon, then God would take care of us on the journey.

As the fall continued, my days smoothed out and life's new sense of normal became more routine. The rhythm of school days and carpools was comfortable now, and the always present piles of laundry were not insurmountable burdens. As we approached baptism weekend in early October, I felt I was strong enough to handle being at church. Enough time had gone by, I figured. Nicholas' baptism would have been back in June, and I was feeling more or less stable emotionally. There was no reason to avoid our church that weekend.

I began to doubt my reasoning as the proud father carried his new infant down the aisle, stopping to allow parishioners to make the sign of the cross on the baby's forehead. Incarnation has seats on three sides of the altar, and we had chosen to sit on the far side of church, as far away from the baptismal font as possible. But now, I realized, that meant I was going to be looking almost straight at the joyful family throughout mass. By the time they had gotten up to take the baby back to the baptismal font, I wanted nothing more than to escape that sanctuary. I was wrong, I can't deal with this! Let me out! But now, the only way out of the church was to walk past the family at the font, with the eyes of the entire congregation focused in one place. Rather than appear rude, I stayed where I was and struggled to hold back the tears for the rest of mass. Perhaps I had farther to go in this journey than I realized.

The week surrounding Nicholas' birthday was a very hard one. I knew it would be difficult, but I was not prepared for the strength with which all those feelings of grief and unfairness came back. It was like reliving those days all over again. The fact that it snowed on December 5th again did not help matters at all. In all my years of living in Virginia, it had never snowed that early in the winter, and here we were with snow on that day for the second year in a row. I will be forever grateful that it snowed on December 5, 2002, for if it had not, Aaron would have been at his weekly aikido class, and I would have been home alone with the boys when I delivered Nicholas. I cannot even begin to imagine what it would have been like to go through Nicholas' birth without Aaron there. That snowfall will forever remain one of the small graces in this experience. But I didn't need to relive that day so closely now!

Having Nicholas' death so closed linked to Matthew's birthday was hard for me, for I anticipated his anniversary at the same time I was trying to prepare to celebrate Matthew turning eight. I was also afraid that Matthew would feel sad as his birthday approached, because of his brother. However, he was only focused on his own excitement. When mention was made of not having been able to go out for his birthday dinner the year before, he asked why. When I reminded him about Nicholas, his reply was a soft "Oh, yeah." How could he not remember, I wondered, after how overshadowed his birthday had been the year before? A year is a long time to a child, I realized, but I still felt hurt that he didn't seem to remember. But my father pointed out to me that Matthew didn't have the sadness as his primary memory of his birthday, because he was remembering the party that we had the day after and all the fun he had then. He hadn't forgotten about Nicholas, but was remembering the day of the party as his birthday. Okay, I thought. Then I had done what I had set out to do by going through with his party the year before—he had a good memory of his birthday, not that his brother had died at that time. Though he would always remember the sadness of losing his brother, he would not always connect Nicholas' death with his birthday, the way I felt I would, and that was good. Since that first year, however, Matthew has mentioned every year how he and Nicholas "share a birthday."

My mother-in-law came to visit shortly before Christmas, and we took her over to the cemetery. It was the first time Mary had been in Charlottesville since Nicholas had died, and it was important to her to visit him with us. The boys cleaned his stone and looked for some small rocks to decorate it, while his grandmother and I just stood there sharing the time. Then Matthew disappeared into the van. When the rest of us got into the car, he was busy writing on a piece of paper. I asked him what he was doing and he told me he'd show it to me when it was done. After we pulled into our driveway, he handed me a small piece of paper with a poem he had written:

As cute as a baby
More precious than diamonds
As soft as a feather,
You are Nicholas, my Holy one.
Happy Birthday, Nicholas, one year old
From your big brother Matthew

In the corner of the paper he had drawn a tiny baby angel. Even though he had not been anticipating the anniversary or had outwardly seemed to dwell on this loss for a long time, this poem told me he was still missing his brother very much.

We didn't have any pictures of Nicholas, having decided it felt weird to take pictures of him in the plastic container. The night before we buried him, we had taken a picture of his small box by one of the flower arrangements we had received, and this we had hanging on our wall of family portraits. When Matthew gave me this poem, I typed it out and framed it together with the photograph in a larger frame. We hung it between the portraits of the older boys as babies.

25

In January 2004, I suspected I might be pregnant, despite our careful charting, and a test at home confirmed it. We wanted to be excited, and in some ways we were. I think Aaron had an easier time being optimistic. But I once again felt I was at the base of a very large mountain. The top was so high up, it was lost in the clouds. There was no way to the top but slowly, one day at a time. Okay, Lord. We are in your hands.

I had an appointment scheduled with Donna for a few weeks later anyway, so we kept that appointment and told her then that we thought I was nine weeks along. Looking at my charts, she said I couldn't possibly be that far along, for my temperature had not jumped up for almost 10 days following the date I indicated as ovulation. However, she had given us the "safe zones" in my cycle, and we had been very careful about them. I knew what the dates were, and an exam and detection of the heartbeat confirmed I was correct.

I had already begun using the progesterone cream, and we continued to walk one day at a time through the very long weeks of the first trimester. Our due date was the 23rd of September, and I couldn't imagine ever reaching the summer, time seemed to move so slowly. How was I going to find the strength to climb this mountain each day when the summit seemed so far away and there was no guarantee of reaching it? Nine months is a long time when you are walking one day at a time.

We had told the boys, family, and close friends even before we had been to see Donna. I knew I needed as many people as possible praying for this baby. Ryan greeted the news with great excitement. At almost four, he was full of things he was going to teach the baby and the anticipation of the fun of being a big brother, much the way Matthew had been during Ryan's pregnancy. Matthew, however, was much more subdued. It was as if he thought that if he didn't get excited, he wouldn't feel pain if something happened to this baby, too. And who could blame him? You told me we were going to have a baby last time, and look what happened! I'm not going to go through that again! Whereas Ryan immediately told all his friends at school, Matthew said he was not going to tell his friends until it was closer to the time the baby would be born, until he really knew he had something to celebrate. Aaron and I both knew from experience that trying not to get excited or attached would not protect him from the pain if something happened this time. But that was how he needed to deal with this new journey and we were going to respect it.

Because what happened with Nicholas was an external event, I was not considered high risk—his pregnancy had been completely normal and healthy. However, one by one, each of the grandparents spoke with us about switching my care to someone else. I know they didn't want to see us have to face any more grief and felt that a different care provider might monitor things more closely or do something differently to help prevent another loss. But we were already doing everything we could do to prevent another first-trimester loss, and there was no way we could have prevented what happened to Nicholas except for not having eaten at that coffee shop that day. I trusted Donna completely—she didn't want to see us face this again either. But neither did she feel we should treat this as anything other than a normal pregnancy, which so far, it was. It was going to be hard to treat it that way emotionally anyway, I didn't need to add extra stress to the journey. Leaving Donna would only have been adding extra stress of being in the care of someone new, not the person who had been through so much with us over the past eight years. Despite concerns from all of our family and numerous friends, I did not get a referral to a specialist or even switch my care to Dr. Wolanski. However, Donna saw me every two weeks instead of every four, at my request. Without being able to feel movement yet, there was no way for me to monitor how the baby was doing. Four weeks was just too long for me to keep the anxiety in check.

Aaron went with me to every check-up this time. I could not stand the thought of possibly facing a problem without him being there. It was only by luck that he had been with me the day Donna had trouble finding Nicholas' heartbeat—I wasn't going to risk being alone if anything happened this time.

At 13 weeks, we went in for a check-up, and everything seemed to be fine. Measurements and weight gain were normal, blood pressure and symptoms were as they had been in the past. Donna got out the Doppler to listen for the heartbeat. Having heard it the past two visits, none of us were too concerned about finding it, but the room got very quiet when she was unable to locate it. As she searched, the anxiety level in the room was growing exponentially the longer the machine voiced just static. After about two minutes, she said, "All right, we are going to ultrasound." Thank God Aaron was with me! There was no way I could have gotten through that morning on my own. I barely held it together while she went to call the hospital, and then she came back with a glass of water for me to drink on the way, and we were sent right over. I looked at her as we left the office and said, "I can't do this again."

She firmly replied, "We are not going to panic until we see the ultrasound."

I leaned on Aaron's arm all the way across the street,

thinking I can't handle this again, Lord! Please, don't make me face this again! I doubt I could have walked across the street on my own. My limbs felt weak and unsteady. Aaron guided me through the hospital doors and into a chair. After we got through registration, we sat and waited, and I drank my water. Barely keeping myself together, I sat gripping Aaron's hand. We sat in silence—what was there we could say to make it any better? He couldn't tell me everything was going to be fine and not to worry, for he was just as scared. Finally, they called us into an exam room. I squeezed Aaron's hand as the technician began the test, and closed my eyes, too scared to look at the monitor. It was no more than a moment or two before the technician said, "Hello, little one." I've heard of people going limp with relief—now I know how it feels. I turned and tried to view the monitor through the tears that were spilling down my cheeks. Aaron pressed his face into my hair as we both tried to calm our pounding hearts. Then we gazed at a heart beating strong and steady on the screen, the tiny arms and legs moving to a music no one else heard. The technician proceeded to do a very detailed ultrasound, measuring and checking everything. All the measurements indicated a healthy baby.

When we got back to Donna's office, she immediately ushered us into a room. The technician had not called her yet to tell her everything was okay, and she had been getting more and more anxious the longer we were there. She had thought they would just do a quick heartbeat check and give her a call. She sat down on the stool and leaned her hands on her knees when we told her all was well. I think we were all feeling a bit weak from the morning's anxieties. When we set up an appointment for two weeks later, I said, "Now, I'm coming every two weeks because you want me to."

"You're darn right, I do!" was her reply.

Needless to say, I was exhausted for the next day or so, drained from the emotional anxiety of that morning. As we told friends and family what had happened, they all had the same reaction: You of all people did not need that! Prior to the next visit, I had a talk with the baby in the parking lot: you need to cooperate this time, please! Don't you do that to me again! I guess it worked, for we never had trouble finding the heartbeat again.

Over the next six months, we lived one day at a time and cautiously checked off each milestone. Getting past the point at which Nicholas died was a big one for me. There was no reason to fear that particular time frame, other than association with Nicholas, but it was a large hurdle emotionally. Even though the progesterone levels had nothing to do with losing Nicholas, Donna decided to keep me on the extra progesterone until we got past the point at which he died. We all knew it wasn't doing anything at that point, for the placenta was providing all the progesterone support the pregnancy needed, but it made us all feel better, and it could do no harm to keep me on it. Donna finally took me off it at about 18 weeks. After I was consistently feeling movement that could be tracked, about 20 weeks, she began to see me every four weeks as in a normal pregnancy.

The pregnancy was a very healthy one, with no issues of concern. My back was not causing me any of the problems it had during Ryan's pregnancy. Aaron checked the level of my pelvic bones each day, and did my physical therapy exercises with me, just to be sure, but the strength training regime I had been doing since Ryan's birth seemed to have done its job. I was walking normally and without pain—physically, at least, this journey was easier. But the top of the mountain still seemed so far away.

We traveled to visit the grandparents as usual during the summer, with Aaron accompanying us on each trip, instead of my driving alone with the boys. The odds of anything bad happening in the third trimester were slim, but everyone, including the extended family, felt safer knowing Aaron was with me. The closer we got to the end of the summer, I began to let myself feel some excitement at the expanding of our family. I had not done any nursery preparations—I just couldn't bring myself to unpack the baby clothes yet. But I was beginning to allow myself to look ahead, and not just live in the moment. Besides, I'd have several weeks to get things ready once the boys went back to school.

At the end of the summer, a friend of mine gave me a flat pewter candle stand engraved with the words:

> The light of God surrounds you
> The love of God enfolds you.
> The power of God protects you.
> The presence of God watches over you.
> Wherever you are, God is.
> Wherever you are, God is.

I decided this was a good mantra to use for labor this time around. I knew they would not let me use an open candle in the hospital, but I would pack the candle holder in my bag anyway, just as a reminder.

Two and a half weeks before my September 23rd due date, I began having contractions. They continued off and on for several days, but they never lasted longer than an hour or so before stopping. At a mid-week check-up with Donna, she told us we were progressing toward labor, and the dilation was beginning. She anticipated that we might not go a full two weeks more, but cautioned that third labors were known for not following the expected course. The boys were just starting back to school—there was still much to do to get ready for this baby! I began to unpack and wash the crib sheets and tiny newborn outfits the boys had worn.

Aaron's aikido dojo was having a seminar that weekend, which began with a pot luck supper on Friday night. As everyone was leaving to go home, the refrain of "see you tomorrow" was repeated as each person left. Then they looked at Aaron and said, "Unless we don't, ha, ha!" With the due date still two weeks away, there was no reason to think he wouldn't be there the next day. I knew differently, however, when I woke up at 6 o'clock the next morning. I let Aaron sleep until 8, to be sure the contractions weren't going to peter out again this time, then woke him and told him he was going to have to miss the seminar.

Aaron took the boys over to Mary Jo, who had agreed to keep them for the day. As Ryan left he gave me a big hug, gave my stomach a kiss and said, "Bye, baby brother or sister!" I took a shower while Aaron was gone, and thought about all the things that were not going to be done as planned before the baby was born. I had not finished with the washing of the baby items. The crib wasn't even set up yet. But this little person did not seem to care that preparations were not complete. Aaron and the boys would have some work to do while I was in the hospital.

With the contractions coming steadily when Aaron got home, we went to meet Donna at her office. I had been two centimeters dilated at the check-up a few days before, so I was distressed to hear her say I was not even four centimeters after four hours of steady labor. I had been feeling the contractions getting stronger, and this news felt like a set back. Since I had not eaten much, she sent us to get a sandwich and told us to check into the hospital after that. I couldn't handle going into a restaurant, so I stayed in the car while Aaron ordered some bagel sandwiches to go.

Things had slowed down considerably by the time we checked into Martha Jefferson, which was even more discouraging. I was able to answer most of the questions without interruption as the nurse went over paper work with me in the delivery room. When she asked if I had a good support system for helping to care for this baby, I thought of all the people who had been praying for us for these long months, weaving the web of support I felt so strongly surrounding me and this little person. I answered "yes" out loud, but thought to myself, "Lady, you have no idea!"

It was a long, unproductive labor, stopping and starting and not progressing for 12 hours—you would think the third time around the body would have a clue what to do! By early afternoon, we were only at five centimeters, and the contractions that had been every two to three minutes earlier in the morning were now coming every ten. I was getting frustrated. We were so close to the top of the mountain—and I still couldn't see the summit.

Donna suggested we break the amniotic sac to get the labor progressing. Once the water breaks, the contractions should pick up in intensity. I was already feeling tired, as much mentally as physically, and part of me dreaded the work that remained ahead of me. But I knew Donna was right when she said leaving things as they were would mean much longer until we were ready for delivery.

She broke the sac, then put me in the jacuzzi tub, in the hopes that the warm water would help ease the pain of the contractions as they increased in intensity. I did a better job of keeping my breathing light this time—not having the excruciating back labor certainly helped. My fingers still got tingly, but they were not going stiff this time, and I focused on my breathing in order to avoid having to use the brown paper bag. As each contraction began, I visualized an angel sitting behind me, supporting me, softly encouraging me: "The light of God surrounds you. The love of God enfolds you." Aaron sponged my face with a cool cloth and fed me ice chips in between contractions, and we tackled each contraction as it came.

After two hours in the tub, Donna got me out to check on the baby's progress. We were at 8 cm. Closer, but still not near the end. And the contractions began to stall out again after I was out of the water. Donna decided to see if walking would pick things up again. We walked the halls of the labor floor, doing laps around the nurses station. The contractions did begin to get into a rhythm again and were getting stronger. I developed a few favorite stopping points along the hallways. As I felt a contraction beginning, I would hurry ahead to my next "comfort spot" to lean on the wall while

Aaron rubbed my back and helped me breathe.

After an hour of walking, Donna checked me again. There was still a small piece of the cervix in the way, and Donna tried to push it back manually during a contraction, having me bear down while she pushed it away. It refused to stay put and I was no longer able to control the breathing during the contractions. But as intense as these contraction were, they were not getting the job done. We were twelve hours into the labor when she told me we needed to start Pitocin.

I stared at her. You have *got* to be kidding me. No, she said. The contractions need to get a little bit stronger in order to fully move that cervix out of the way, and they just aren't doing it on their own. We can either start Pitocin and be done with this in an hour, or we can remain at this level of intensity for several more unproductive hours. My face must have shown how defeated I felt at that point, for she offered me an epidural. I knew from childbirth classes that nine centimeters was past the point at which they would usually do them, for it takes a while for it to work and would take a long time to wear off. Donna doesn't like to use them and her expression told me it wasn't really what she wanted to do at this point. However, she also could tell I had very little strength left. We decided on a pain killer in the IV instead, which should have taken the edge off the pain. But it did nothing to counter the drug induced contractions.

I had nothing left to draw from after thirteen hours, and Donna had to talk me through the pushing contractions. She tried to keep me focused on the peaceful beach scene painted on the wall behind her, but the wall kept dissolving into a gray cloud with each contraction. I was afraid I was going to pass out, so I kept my eyes shut. Like the pregnancy, the delivery was a long ordeal, but at 7:13pm on September 11, 2004, the journey finally came to an end. Tristan Andrew was in our arms, a healthy 7 pounds 11 ounces.

Dr. Klas came to the hospital right after Tristan was born, to check him out. We were surprised to see him so soon, and he explained he had been out to dinner with his wife and had stopped on the way back home. Evidently, the hospital had called him earlier in the day to tell him I was in labor, but he had not heard back from them. He decided to stop to see how things were going, and was there to meet Tristan less than an hour after he was born. When I told him the next day how much his visit had meant to us, he said he had been thinking of us all day and didn't want to miss seeing this baby. He said, "Every child is a gift—but some have more bows than others."

The whole family was on hand six weeks later when we baptized Tristan on October 24, 2004. We went to the cemetery on the way home from church, the first time all of the extended family had been there together. It was very important to me for all of us to go that day, for Nicholas was very much a part of Tristan's life, and his reason for being. It was quite a mix of emotions to stand at the grave of one son, holding another, knowing he would not exist but for that grave. My heart still ached for the child I couldn't hold, but no longer could I say I would go back and change it if I could, for that same heart was filled with the joy of this beautiful new baby. Tristan cannot and will not ever take the place of Nicholas, but he is living proof that the sun does indeed shine again. He has brought such joy into our family, and I can't imagine our lives without him.

In December, Aaron and I performed with the Festival choir in the annual Advent concert. As I stood on the risers and sang:

> A time will come for singing
> When all your tears are shed
> When sorrow's chains are broken
> And broken hearts shall mend

I was struck by the power of those words. Two years earlier, as a member of the congregation, the song had had me in tears. Now I could see Peggy in the audience, my new

son curled against her shoulder, and smile.
   A time had come for singing.

26

At least for a while.

I immersed myself in raising my boys, watching Tristan grow and seeing the delight he brought to the entire family. Though my heart still ached for Nicholas, I treasured the gift of my rainbow after the storm.

As Tristan grew through preschool and I approached the end of my thirties, I slowly began to pass on to others things that he outgrew. Though Aaron and I had not made a conscious decision that our family was complete, the more years that passed the more I felt that that window was closing. It had been a difficult road into motherhood, and I could be content with my three beautiful boys.

But in January of 2011, I found myself staring down at two dark lines in the window of a pregnancy test.

Really?? I stared at the stick, not really blinking. Then I looked heavenward.

Really?!?

I was two months shy of my 42nd birthday. Seriously, Lord?? What are you thinking?

It's not that I was opposed to more children. But I was over 40 and had already lost four babies. The odds were not in my favor.

Lord, I can't face losing another baby. I'm not sure I could put my heart together again. I'm not sure I can do this. I'm going to have to trust that You will take care of me and this little one. This is in Your hands.

Aaron and I both walked around in kind of a daze for several weeks. The thought of starting all over again with diapers and sleep deprivation was overwhelming. After all, Matthew was in high school. Tristan was in first grade and I finally had some time to myself for the first time in fifteen years.

I called Donna and she set up an ultrasound appointment and a blood draw, just to be sure all was well. She would see me in a few weeks.

We told the boys before we told anyone else. We were going to need a good support system to walk the long journey of this pregnancy, and we felt it only right that the boys should know first. Tristan was immediately excited at the thought of becoming a big brother. We had figured he would be excited, but expected that Matthew, at 15, would be more embarrassed than anything. "Are you kidding? My parents are having a baby?" But he was almost as excited as Tristan. "When can I tell my friends?", he wanted to know. We asked him to wait for a while before sharing the news, to be sure things were going to be alright. Ryan remained quiet. His look was almost one of concern of being replaced. Why the new guy? it said. You're not happy with my work?

Once the boys knew, we slowly shared the news with family and friends. My friend Peggy also has a son who is much younger than his siblings. I knew if anyone would understand how I was feeling it was her. When I told her, in the middle of a crowed restaurant, she took my hand and said, "Jeremiah 29:11"

"What?" That was not a verse with which I was familiar.

"Jeremiah 29:11. 'I know the plan I have for you says the Lord.'"

But...I'm scared. What if....

Peggy could see all the doubt in my eyes. She patted my hand again. "I know the plan I have for you says the Lord.

It's going to be okay."

I wanted to believe her. But the mountain loomed high in the clouds and I just couldn't imagine the journey again.

Later that week, I went to an appointment with my primary physician. I had not yet told them we were expecting again. I figured I would do so at this asthma check up. The nurse who called me back greeted me at the door by saying, "How are you doing, mamma?"

"How did you know?" I asked.

She smiled. "The hospital sent us your ultrasound report. How are you feeling about all this?" I looked at her with eyes overwhelmed by it all. She went about taking my vitals and said, "You and I are the same age, and I know how I would feel in this situation. How are you doing ?"

"I'm scared," I admitted. "Trying not to give into the anxiety."

She stopped taking my blood pressure. "Jeremiah 29:11"

"I know the plan I have for you says the Lord." I said.

She nodded.

"You are the second person to quote me that verse this week," I told her.

"Then you need to listen. It's going to be okay."

She was right. I have to trust that God has given us this child for a reason and that He will take care of it. And me.

All medical indications were that everything was fine. The blood work came back with hormone levels in the perfect range, the ultrasound had shown a normal 7 week embryo. But still when I went for my first checkup with Donna a few weeks later, I asked her when I would get over the anxiety.

"You won't." I blinked. "I'm not going to sugarcoat this for you," she said. My age and our history compounded the risks of miscarriage. "We are one day at a time." Of course, that is the only way any of us can live any part of our lives, really. But one day at a time sounds very long when you stand at the base of the mountain.

Although the baby was healthy, the pregnancy turned out

to be a difficult one. The first trimester nausea hit hard, usually in the mid afternoon, just about the time I had to drive across town to pick up the boys from school. I never got sick, but the dry heaves often plagued me for much of the car ride. Brushing my teeth would make me gag. Cooking was almost impossible, though I was usually able to pick at my dinner. And the fatigue was almost crushing some days. Thank goodness it gets better after the first trimester, I thought, holding on to the notion of only a few more weeks. But it didn't get better. The symptoms persisted past the fourth month, gradually easing, but not really disappearing until almost to the halfway point.

One of the first people to find out our news was my orthopedist. I had been coping with a soft tissue problem in my right wrist for some time, and shortly before Thanksgiving he had tried a steroid shot. At the time, he told me one of three things would happen: I would never need to come in again, I would come back in a few years to repeat the shot, or I'd be back in his office in two months. If that was the case, the only remaining option would be to surgically fix the problem. Here I was, back in his office, so we both knew we were out of options. I told him the discomfort was interfering with life, especially being my dominant hand—but since I had seen him last, we had found out I was pregnant. He gave me a big congratulatory hug and told me not to worry. Once we got into the second trimester, he could operate on my wrist without risk to the baby. They would only need to use a local anesthesia and they would monitor the baby via ultrasound both before and after the surgery. I would just need to cope with the discomfort until we got past the fourth month.

In the middle of April, I went into the outpatient surgery center to have my wrist fixed. My parents accompanied me so Aaron could save as much vacation time as possible for later in the year. As promised, they checked on the baby before the surgery with an ultrasound, and the OB team felt there was no risk to going ahead. I remained awake through the whole procedure, so there was little to recover from in the post op area. After they had given me something to eat and drink, they took me back downstairs for another ultrasound check. I invited my parents to come in and watch. My father declined, but my mother came with me. It was the first time she had ever seen an ultrasound, and she was in awe of the detail that could be seen. This little one seemed unperturbed by the events of the morning, and we were told we were fine to go home.

That same month the nausea began to go away. Finally, I can start really feeling better, I thought. But around that time, my blood pressure dropped. I have always had blood pressure on the low end of normal, but this was low even for me, and left me feeling light headed and tired a good portion of the time. I didn't think that was very fair—the second trimester is when you are supposed to get your energy back and feel good! One Sunday in church as the congregation stood up for the Gospel the light-headedness got particularly strong. I didn't stand. But even sitting wasn't enough. I leaned forward, resting my head in my hands. Aaron leaned down to see if I was okay. I shook my head. Do you want me to walk you out? No, if I tried to stand up I thought I would pass out. He sat down next to me and I lay my head in his lap throughout the sermon. When I felt I could safely stand, he led me to the sofa in the entryway. One of our friends from the choir is an EMT, and Aaron went back in to ask her to come have a look at me. She checked my blood pressure and had Aaron get me some water. The color was coming back into my face by that point, and she said she thought I was fine, but should check in with my physician just to be sure. When I called Donna later she told me I should keep a juice box and some pretzels in my purse, and anytime I felt like that I should immediately lay down, no matter where I was. There was no harm to the baby from the low blood pressure —but a fall from passing out would be a different story.

Around this point I also began to have extreme sensitivity to florescent lights. Within minutes of walking into a place like Walmart, I would begin feeling dizzy and nauseous. I started to avoid going into brightly lit stores if at all possible, and wearing sunglasses while shopping if I absolutely had to go into one.

The physical demands of this pregnancy were draining, but the emotional strain was equally so. With every week that passed, the worry over losing the baby eased a tiny bit, but still I wrestled with anxiety. Getting past the first trimester was once again the first big milestone, but having already experienced the death of a baby in the second trimester, I knew we would not fully relax with this pregnancy any more than we did with Tristan's. And I was seven years older than when I was pregnant with Tristan. So much more could go wrong.

I continued to feel like the road had taken a sudden detour and the new path we were on didn't seem quite real. My boys were getting more independent, I had the chance to pursue some of my own dreams and now suddenly those were being put on hold indefinitely again. Once when a friend asked me how I was doing, I told her that maybe someday God would explain to me why the road suddenly took a sharp turn.

"Or maybe," she said gently, "the road has always gone this way and you just couldn't see around the curve."

She was right. Just because this pregnancy wasn't part of my plan, didn't make it not part of a greater one.

Jeremiah 29:11.

Because of my age, Donna sent me to a high risk specialist for additional maternal testing. At 13 weeks, they had drawn blood and done an ultrasound. A few days later, a technician called to tell me that the tests indicated a greater than 1 in 5 chance that our baby could have Down's Syndrome. My anxiety skyrocketed. I knew I would love this baby, no matter what, but the thought of going through this unexpected and difficult pregnancy to then raise a special needs child was

145

overwhelming. Friends kept reminding me that 1 in 5 means there is a 4 in 5 chance there won't be a problem and I tried to hold on to that and trust that all would be okay, but it was hard. Looking back on it, I never would have agreed to that test had I know the level of anxiety we would live with for the next ten weeks.

For our 22 week ultrasound, we went back to the same high risk doctor. Many people had been saying "I bet you are hoping for a girl." and although we had not found out the gender before hand with any of the boys, we decided this time we wanted to know. Part of me was hoping for a girl, for this was the last opportunity we would have and I did not want to have disappointment be an emotion in the delivery room, should it turn out we were to have another son. As I pulled into the parking lot for that ultrasound, I suddenly knew. It's a boy. I felt like an angel had whispered the news in my ear, so I would be prepared. Sure enough, when the technician took a look, she said, "You have a son."

She took her time and did careful measurement of all parts of our little boy. Everything looked to be on track for a healthy baby. Then the doctor came in and did the ultrasound all over again, measuring the length of the thigh bone, the fold at the back of the neck, the nasal bone—all the physical markers for Down's Syndrome. With every measurement he took, he said, "Good, good, that looks normal." At the end of the ultrasound, though he of course could not say with 100% certainty, he told us that all appears normal and the chance of Down's Syndrome was very low.

At our follow up appointment with Donna she read through the report with us. With the exception of his nasal bone, which appeared on the small side, all the other markers for Down's appeared normal. Donna looked at us and said, "We don't know the length of the other boys' nasal bones, for they were never measured. For that matter, we don't know the length of either of yours! This baby is fine." A little bit more breath could be released. One more milestone down.

As we began to tell people we were having another boy and many people asked if I was disappointed not to be having a girl. In a small way, I was, for as much as I love my boys, I would also have loved to experience having a daughter. I voiced this to a friend of mine, who smiled and acknowledged she could understand that.

"But you are raising good men. And the world needs more good men. So God chose you to raise another."

What a beautiful way of looking at this unexpected gift.

Now that we knew the gender of the baby, we started talking about names. I figured we would go back to the name books and go through the process we had used with the older boys, but this time skipping the girls names. Before we had really begun that process, the boys started chiming in with their own ideas.

Balthazar, Matthew suggested. Um, a world of no.

"Oh come on, Mom, Balthazar is a great name!"

"Then you can use if for your first son. I am not naming your baby brother Balthazar."

Our favorite boys' names had already been used, so this was going to require more discussion. Aaron liked James, but I knew too many little boys names James. There were two in Tristan's class of 17 for starters. No, I didn't want something that was being used too frequently. The boys continued to throw out their own ideas, until one of them said, "How about Griffin?"

"Yeah! Griffin."

Griffin? Yes, I like that one. It was definitely a possibility. But Aaron was reluctant. Over the next few weeks, the boys kept urging their father to agree, badgering him even.

"Come on, Dad. It's a great name! You know it is."

Eventually, they just started referring to the baby as Griffin. I kept reminding them that it wasn't their decision and their father needed to have a say in the name choice. "You shouldn't call him Griffin—you don't know that that is his name," I told them one day at lunch. Tristan looked at me with an oh-come-on look on his face and said matter of factly, "Yes, it is, Mom."

Okay, I told them. You need to come up with some good reasons why you think that should be your brother's name. Don't just badger Dad, give him some concrete reasons. So the three of them had an earnest discussion over lunch. At dinner that night, they presented their case to their father. They told him that Griffin was a strong name, a different name, unusual without being weird. Aaron told them he would take their opinions under advisement. But he remained unconvinced.

In addition to the ultrasound, at the mid point of the pregnancy it was time for the gestational diabetes test. Gestational diabetes effects women of all ages, but the older the mother and the more pregnancies she has had, the higher the risk. It is a temporary condition, usually resolving as soon as the baby is born, but carries the same risks and problems as regular diabetes, with blood sugar levels not being well controlled by the body's normal insulin production. It can lead to high blood pressure in the mother as well as heavier than normal birth weights in babies, which in turn can lead to increased risk of c-section. It can also effect the infant's respiratory system and own ability to regulate insulin. Because it often shows no symptoms, all expectant mothers are routinely tested. The expectant mother arrives at the hospital having had nothing to eat or drink from the night before besides water. A blood sample is drawn and then she is required to drink 8oz of a super sugary liquid. After an hour, the blood draw is repeated, to see how her body is metabolizing the liquid. If her blood glucose levels are elevated, she is at a higher risk for the disease, and more testing is required.

I dreaded this test every pregnancy. The drink is like an orange soda, which I don't care for anyway, only about ten times as sweet. And thicker. I had had to choke it down the previous times and it made my stomach nauseous. I was not looking forward to it.

I had always passed the first screen without any trouble, but this time, the glucose levels were elevated. Now I had to endure the three hour version of this test. The procedure is the same, but the blood draws occur at 1, 2 and 3 hours after drinking the solution. You are not allowed to eat until after the third one, and you are not allowed to leave the hospital, since the blood must be drawn at exactly those marks. My mother came with me, to keep me company. This time the solution was more like Sprite, which made it slightly more palatable. But only slightly. Because I had been experiencing light-headedness already in this pregnancy, Donna was concerned how I would handle this extended period without food. On her orders, as soon as the three hour blood draw was over, we went straight to the cafeteria for breakfast.

The three hour test gave ambiguous results. My glucose levels were elevated at one draw but not the other two. Not enough of problem to diagnose full blown diabetes, but enough to warrant monitoring. Donna urged me to be extra careful about my diet and monitored my blood pressure carefully at each visit.

As the spring moved toward summer, the question became where is the baby going to sleep? Our three bedroom house was built in the early 1970's, and the bedrooms are small. Our master bedroom did not have enough room for a crib. We can't put the baby in with the high schooler, and he didn't want to go back to sharing a room with Ryan. And we couldn't put the baby in with the soon to be seven year old, for there were always Legos everywhere. Where is the baby going to sleep turned into renovating 80% of the house.

Major renovation projects are overwhelming in the best of times. Everything from the lower level of the house, the kitchen and living room had to be moved to a storage pod in the driveway. Even though it was just a renovation, the process was the same as if we were moving across the country. Being six months pregnant with ongoing light-headedness and fatigue made the packing process all the more exhausting.

Our contractor had promised us the whole project would be finished in six weeks. Not possible, everyone told us. You'll be living at your parents for months. But we didn't have that kind of time. This project must be finished before this baby is born.

We came home from a trip to New York at the beginning of August back into our own home, newly completed and wonderful—and a complete wreck. Everything we had moved to the storage pod in the driveway now needed to be put away. It was just like having moved into a new house, except we had only moved to the driveway and back. There were boxes upon boxes to be unpacked. I need this all put away, I thought. I can't bring a baby home into this chaos. However, the light-headedness had not gone away, and there was only so much being on my feet that I could handle.

A week after we got home, I began to have contractions. I was only 35 weeks, but having gone through labor three times before, I knew these were not just Braxton-Hicks contractions, for they were definitely doing the "longer, stronger, closer together" progression. After about five hours, I called Donna and we met her in her office. She did a manual exam and told me the cervix was tight and closed—nothing was happening. Nothing productive anyway. They were real contractions, just not actually accomplishing anything.

She got out the Doppler to check his heartbeat. She started to look concerned as she couldn't find it. I could feel him moving, so I wasn't too worried, but still she couldn't get a reading. He had been head down for about two weeks, so she was searching where his heart ought to be, but then began to move the wand around to other parts of my abdomen. All at once she got a clear reading of a steady, strong heartbeat—but not where near where it should have been if he were still head down. Donna did a physical exam of my abdomen and discovered that the baby had not only pulled back up from resting on the cervix, he was now laying crosswise.

Donna could tell I was looking downhearted. We don't want him to come now, she reminded me. He's not ready yet. I knew that, but my body was so tired. The thought of another month before delivery was exhausting.

She told me to take a warm bath and have a glass of wine with dinner. If that didn't quiet things down, she gave me a prescription for Percocet. Really? Percocet? It will calm the contractions, she told me, and let you sleep.

We went home with instructions to stay off my feet. She didn't put me officially on bed rest, but I was under strict instructions to be off my feet as much as possible. Let the boys unpack, she told me. You are not to lift anything. Can I do things from sitting down, I wondered. If they bring me boxes can I shelve books and things like that? She shook her head. You sit on the couch with your feet up, she told me. Or I will put you on bed rest.

Even after the warm bath and the wine with dinner, by 8pm the contractions appeared to be getting stronger again. And I was exhausted. Reluctantly, I decided to take one of the pills—only one, which was half the dose she prescribed. Aaron was watching a movie with the boys downstairs and I headed to bed. Within ten minutes, I felt like I was in the middle of Dorothy's tornado. The entire house seemed to be rotating around my head. I lay with my eyes closed and still the room was spinning. For over an hour I lay there not moving, feeling that if I moved an arm or a leg I would fly across the room.

Aaron tiptoed into the room after the boys were in bed, and he must have heard me make a sound for he came over to the bed.

"I'm sorry I woke you."

"I wasn't asleep," I whispered in a small voice.

He leaned down next to the bed. "What's wrong?"

"The whole house is spinning," I whimpered. Aaron went

around to his side of the bed and lay down behind me. He put his arm over me and stroked my hair with his other hand.

"There's nothing we can do. We just have to wait for it to wear off." He lay there like that, not sleeping, just anchoring me to the bed, for the next three hours. His arm over me helped me feel like I would not fly across the room, but it was a long, horrible three hours. Gradually the meds left my system and the room began to steady. I decided those types of drugs were never going into my body again.

As if she knew how overwhelmed I felt at all there was to do with putting the house back in order, my best friend from childhood had called the week before to say she wanted to come down from DC and help me for a day or two. I gratefully made a date for her to visit, and it could not have been better timed. The day after the house spinning experience, Jill and her teenage son arrived with a cooler full of food. She had everything all ready for dinner that evening. When I told her about the pre-term labor, she looked around the house and said, "Okay, boys, let's get to work!" She immediately began giving all four boys jobs to do, and they did whatever she asked. They moved boxes, put books on shelves, carried furniture around, and made great progress in taming the chaos from the move. We had just finished moving Matthew to his new bedroom downstairs and Tristan and Ryan to Matthew's old room, but the vacated room needed cleaning and painting. Jill swept and dusted and covered all the murals on the walls with paper so the walls could be repainted. She was only there for a day and a half, but the house looked so much better when she left. And even though I spent most of her visit on the couch, she had lifted my spirits by taking such good care of me as well as the house. Her visit was a ray of sunshine in the haze of fatigue.

My goal had been to get everyone settled back into school and then I would have a week or two to get the baby's room and things ready. But the night before the first day of school, I went into labor again. We arranged for a friend to pick the boys up the next morning and after another six hours of contractions growing longer, stronger, closer together, we went to meet Donna. Because it was late at night and I was now 37 weeks, she met us at the hospital and took us to a triage room.

Once again, everything was tight and closed. Are you kidding me? I've now endured a total of twelve hours of labor and we haven't even started yet? I know, it's still early, but how many times are we going to do this?

After the last round of labor, the baby had settled back into a head down position. But when Donna checked for the heartbeat, he was once again back up and rotated, as he had been two weeks before. Donna shook her head. "Well, he's obviously not ready." I asked why he kept pulling back up. "I don't know," she said. "But he's not going to have room to turn back around if he keeps this up."

The boys had their first week of school and I had a quiet week at home—except I wasn't allowed to do any of the preparations that still needed doing. Aaron and Matthew had gotten the room painted, but the crib wasn't assembled, the baby clothes weren't washed. And all I was allowed to do was sit and read. On the one hand, it was the last chance I was going to have for quiet time to myself. But it left me feeling frustrated at my limitations. And the rest did nothing to alleviate the crushing fatigue.

I went to bed early Thursday night, but woke up uncomfortable after a few hours. I got up and started walking around. Aaron joined me, and after several very strong contractions, he asked me if I wanted him to call Donna. Not yet. I was not going to go to the hospital only to be sent home again. I paced the house, going from the living room to the baby's bedroom and back again. Leaning on the kitchen counters or rocking in the nursery rocking chair, I breathed through hour after hour of contractions.

By 5am they were coming every three minutes or so and had definitely increased in intensity. Donna said she's see us at hospital at 6. At 5:30, we called my parents and asked them to come over and get everyone through the morning routine. The boys were all asleep, so we left a note on the kitchen table telling them we had gone to the hospital and that their grandparents would be there at 7:30 to take them to school. Then off we headed to Martha Jefferson for the third time in as many weeks.

On the way, I said, "You know, we should probably decide on a name for this little person." Aaron had been holding out for James, despite my protestations of it being too common a name right then, so name discussions had not really progressed in the past few weeks.

Aaron glanced at me sheepishly. "I think they've gotten to me. I've been thinking of him as Griffin."

I smiled. "Do you want to use James as a middle name?"

He shook his head. Griffin James Olowin didn't flow well. We decided upon Christopher. Griffin Christopher—a strong name, unusual without being weird. Yes, the boys would be happy with that.

Once again Donna met us in the triage room. This time I was 4cm dilated. She smiled. "Want to have a baby today?"

Oh, thank goodness.

I had decided early on in this pregnancy that I wanted to have an epidural. Except for the ineffective IV pain med I was given with the Pitocin in Tristan's delivery, I had not had any medications of any kind with the other three deliveries. But Tristan's delivery had been so hard, and I didn't think I could go through that again. When I had gone for my postpartum checkup after he was born, I had told Donna I thought I had been close to passing out from the pain. She assured me that was unlikely.

"You know that beautiful beach scene on the wall behind your head in the delivery room?" I asked.

She nodded.

"It wasn't there towards the end. There was nothing but gray mist and your face."

She raised her eyebrows. "Wow, you were close to passing out."

People say women forget about the level of pain of labor after the baby is born. But I remembered Tristan's delivery very clearly and I was very reluctant to go through that again. Besides, I've done natural childbirth three times already. I had nothing to prove, and this pregnancy had been long and draining. Let's take this delivery a little easier.

Between the triage room and labor and delivery, I had to stop more than once at a wall to breathe through a contraction. Are you ready for that epidural, Donna wondered.

Definitely.

The hospital was brand new, having just moved from the original building to this location on Monday of that week. The birthing rooms were large and light colored, with windows overlooking the Blue Ridge mountains in the distance. The facility was lovely, but the staff was still figuring out where things like tissues were kept and how the fancy lighting system worked. But none of that worried me. After being up all night, the best thing about the room to me was the bed.

As soon as they were able, they got the anesthesiologist into my room to administer the epidural. By 7:30, the nurses had me hooked up to an IV and a fetal heart monitor and the doctor had inserted the epidural. Relief should come fairly quickly, they told me. Because epidurals tend to slow labor progress a bit, Donna decided to administer Pitocin in the IV. With the pain blocked by the medication, the harder contractions wouldn't be an issue, and we'd get through this process faster.

Donna saw me settled into the bed and then excused herself to go reschedule her morning appointments. Her office was in the same complex as the hospital, a five minute walk down the hill. She assured me she would be back in an hour. Even with the Pitocin, we were still several hours away from delivery at best. She'd be back in plenty of time, and could return in less than 10 minutes if the staff needed to contact her. Rest for a while, she told me

At first the epidural seemed to be doing its job. By comparison to what I had been feeling, the contractions were significantly less painful. Except for a two inch wide strip down the left side of my abdomen, which was not going numb. The Pitocin was beginning to kick up the intensity of the contractions, and I was feeling every bit in that two inch strip. But I was strapped to machines and my legs were numb, so there was little I could do to manage it except rock back and forth. The nurse tried turning me on my left side, hoping the medicine would "seep" over to the area, but nothing worked. I felt I would have been better off without the medication, for at least then I'd be able to walk, use the whirlpool and find other ways of working through each contraction. But I was trapped in the bed.

After a while of trying to help me manage this, the nurse excused herself to go find the anesthesiologist. "He needs to adjust this—this is not what you signed up for." Definitely not.

With all three of the other boys, my water had not broken on its own. So it was a little surprising when it broke shortly after the nurse left the room. Everything was wet, so Aaron pushed the nurse's call button, to get some help with changing sheets and gowns.

Unbeknownst to us, when Donna had left she had privately told the nurse that if my water broke she was to check for the umbilical cord. Because the baby had pulled up and sideways with each preterm labor, Donna was worried about the cord prolapsing—coming down the birth canal before the baby's head. When that happens, the cord can become compressed and cut off oxygen to the baby, necessitating emergency surgery.

Also unbeknownst to us, some of the alarms had been incorrectly wired at the nurse's station. So when Aaron pushed the normal nurses' call button, a "code red" type of emergency alarm rang at the nurses' station. Our nurse had been in the OR, alerting the anesthesiologist to our need of attention, and as she was coming back past the nurses station was told her patient was in distress. She came flying into the room, looking like the devil himself was on her heels.

"What's wrong??"

Aaron was surprised at the urgency in her voice. "Her water broke. Everything is all wet."

Because she had been instructed by Donna to check for the cord, the nurse was inwardly concerned that this could still be an emergency situation, but so as not to alarm us, she calmly said, "Well, let's take this opportunity to find out how things are progressing."

She donned a glove and did an physical check. And got a strange look on her face. She frowned. "Hmm..."

Hmm, what?

She frowned again. "I think I feel a nose."

What?

She took off the glove and said, "I'm going to call Donna."

She went out of the room and left us feeling a little uneasy. And with everything still wet. Although my legs were numb, I could still feel the heavy clamminess of wet sheets.

Ten minutes later, Donna came into the room, pulling on a glove as she entered. "Well, I hear someone's being ornery. Let's see what's going on."

It was only a few seconds before she said, "I just put my finger in his mouth. We're done."

In his mouth? What does that mean?

"He's in a full facial presentation." She put her hand up to her face, with her pinky on her forehead and her thumb on her chin. "He's trying come come this way."

"So, we need a C-section?"

She nodded. "This isn't safe. We're done."

She left the room to find Dr. Wolanski, who was already

on the floor prepping for a scheduled C-section. Aaron stroked my hand as we tried to absorb this new news. This was definitely an abrupt turn of events.

A few minutes later, she was back in the room. "He's on his way down." Then she looked at me with a serious expression. "He'd going to try and tell you he can turn this baby. I'm telling you there isn't room. Don't let him talk you into it."

It was about 9am when Dr. Wolanski came in about 10 minutes later. He did a physical check and also poked Griffin in the mouth, confirming a full facial presentation.

"We can let labor continue," he said. "And I can try and push him back up the birth canal a bit and attempt to rotate his head back into the proper presentation."

That didn't sound like much fun for either me or the baby, even with the epidural. And Donna was standing behind Dr. Wolanski, shaking her head back and forth emphatically.

"Are we likely to end up with a C-section in a few hours anyway?" I asked.

"That is fairly likely, yes."

Then why on earth would I put both of us through that, I thought. Donna was still shaking her head at me from behind him. I know he was giving me the choice because I had had three natural births already. And women who work with midwives generally want as little intervention as possible. But I knew too many stories of loss. Natural birth was not my priority.

"I can't risk losing this baby, Ed. He's not in distress. Get him out before that happens."

"Alright." He turned to the nurses. "Ten minutes we are in the OR."

The nurse shook her head at me as he walked out. "45. There's no way we can have you ready in 10."

People began bustling about. Drugs had to be administered to stop the labor, my stomach scrubbed and disinfected, forms had to be signed. Bags of fluids and antibiotics were added to the IV already in my hand. Then we needed to have a conversation with the new anesthesiologist, who would take the epidural to a full spinal block for surgery. When she heard the story of the epidural that didn't work and the new turn of events, she expressed gentle sympathy to me.

"This was not how you planned on this delivery going, was it?"

No, it wasn't.

"You expected a quiet, manageable experience for once."

I nodded.

"But, it seems you are not destined to have that."

No. But the most important thing was to have Griffin safely in the world. She agreed and more forms were signed.

Almost exactly 45 minutes after the decision was made, they wheeled me into the operating room. Once they had me settled and hooked to all the monitors, Aaron and Donna, both in masks and gowns, were allowed into the room. They placed a stool by my head and had Aaron sit and hold the hand that was not strapped down with IV's. Donna positioned herself where she could see around the drape that prevented us from watching the surgery.

Just as Dr. Wolanski said, "Okay, here we go.", our new family physician, Kurt Elward, walked into the OR. The hospital had alerted him that I had been admitted, and Donna had called to tell him of the impending C-section. He arrived just in time to take his place next to where the newborn is examined.

The actual delivery part of a C-section happens very quickly. The majority of the time in the OR is the careful sewing together of the many layers of muscle that have been cut. Dr. Wolanski lifted Griffin into the arms of a waiting nurse, who brought him swiftly over to Dr. Elward. Though I couldn't see them except from the corner of my eye, Kurt spoke aloud as he examined our crying son.

"Looks good. He looks good, Mom."

Within a few minutes, while they were just beginning the

process of closing everything back up, Kurt handed the now swaddled Griffin to Aaron, who held him close to my face so I could see him. I couldn't hold him, but Aaron positioned him where I could touch his head with my one free hand. Two beautiful little eyes blinked at me, and brought tears to my own. The journey to the top of this mountain had been long and full of rocky slopes. But we had made it.

Griffin weighed in at 8lbs 12oz, ten ounces more than Ryan, who until that time had been the heaviest of my sons. While I was in recovery, Aaron came in from the nursery where he had accompanied Griffin to be weighed and washed. When he told me how much he weighed I was astounded. Really? Yep. Aaron and Donna had asked the nurse to reweigh him, because neither of them believed it either.

Donna came to my room during evening rounds that night, even though I was technically Dr. Wolanski's patient at that point. She sat chatting with us and agreed that he weighed much more than she had anticipated. "I don't know where you were hiding 8lbs, 12 oz. It was all baby."

"So we were likely to end up with a C-section anyway, weren't we?" I asked.

She nodded. "Yes, most likely." Then she turned serious. "I had a feeling this one wasn't going to go smoothly. There was just a feeling in my gut that told me this wasn't going to be normal."

We asked what she meant, and she told us of her concerns about the cord prolapse, and of just being on edge after he pulled back up in the multiple preterm labor episodes. Then she looked at the two of us.

"Did Ed tell you the cord was around the neck?"

"No." I'm sure I went pale.

She nodded slowly. She could see over the curtain as Griffin was being delivered, and had seen Dr. Wolanski deliver the baby's head, gently lift the umbilical cord from around his neck, and lift him fully out.

"So, if we had tried to push him back..."

"Bad. It would have been bad." We would have compressed the cord, I realized. And we could have lost him in delivery. She locked eyes with me. "This little one was trying to tell us things couldn't happen the usual way."

The journey to the top of the mountain had been long and challenging. Though the view from the top was of my four beautiful boys, the physical exhaustion ran very deep, and it was months before I began to feel I was recovering.

One day when Griffin was about six months old, I impulsively stopped into a local Christian bookstore located in a mall where I had other errands to do. While browsing the shelves of knick knacks, I came upon a pewter picture frame that read "Journey...Trust in the Lord." Along one side of the photo opening were the words "He will guide your paths." and on the other side "Seek His will in all you do." Across the bottom was quoted "For I know the plans I have for you," says the Lord. "...plans for good...to give you a future and a hope."

Jeremiah 29:11.

I brought the frame home and placed in it the photo that we used for Griffin's birth announcements, of the three older boys all leaning in around the sleeping newborn, smiling at the camera with delight. No matter how old my boys get, that photo will always remain the one in that frame, a reminder of comfort and strength given to me on the journey.

Epilogue

For certain I would never have chosen to walk this journey. It has not been an easy road to follow and not something anyone would ever plan to do. And yet, as I look back, I can see how the person I am today is different from who I would have been at this stage in my life if I had not suffered through those four losses. Losing a baby changes you forever. You can never go back to who you were before it happened. You have to come to find and understand the new person you are. Those experiences are a part of who I am, and I am stronger because of them. Whatever else life brings my way, I will handle differently because of my children—all of them.

I know my four little angles in Heaven will always be a part of our family, most especially Nicholas, who touched so many people with his short little life. I believe that they are waiting for me and I will get to know them all when my journey on this earth is complete. But until then, there will always be a part of my heart that aches for them. Perhaps someday, God will explain all of this to me, but for now, I just have to remember the words of a poem I read after Nicholas died:

> My life is but a weaving,
> between my Lord and me
> I cannot choose the colors,
> He weaveth steadily.
> Ofttimes he weaveth sorrow,
> and I in foolish pride,
> Forget He sees the upper,

and I the underside.
Not 'til the loom is silent
and the shuttles cease to fly,
Shall God unroll the canvas
and explain the reason why.
The dark threads are as needful
in the skillful Weaver's hand
As the threads of gold and silver
in the pattern He has planned.
 -Author unknown

Journeying Forward

About four months after Nicholas died, we received word of a day long workshop for bereaved parents, being held at a church about an hour from our house. Friends kept the boys for us and we spent the day in the presence of other bereaved parents, focusing on our grief journey. There were speakers, small group discussions, quiet spaces and a memorial mass, all offered within the safe space of people who understood. I found it to be very helpful, for it was the first time I was in the presence of others living through this same surreal experience, and it brought home the fact that there are other people coping with this same loss, no matter how alone I felt.

I came home from that day feeling that I wanted to participate in bringing that kind of comfort to others, and our pastor told me I had his support for whatever I needed. In the years before Griffin was born, I offered one or two workshops per year, both at our church and as a guest speaker and facilitator at other churches in the area. I told my own story, offered resources of support and facilitated sharing among those who wished to do so. Some of these were attended by as few as two people, others by a dozen, but each time I tried to provide safe space to be wherever the participants were on their own personal journey.

After Griffin was born, I stopped offering the workshops, not because they are no longer needed, but because they were simply too much work for one person to continue to offer alone. But I did not want to stop offering the help to others, and since 2014, I have been helping to facilitate a monthly support group at our local hospital.

This book originally stemmed from my attempts to write out my own story to present at the workshops. In not wanting to forget anything that might be helpful to someone else to hear, I realized there was far more I wanted to say than could fit into a 20-30 minute talk. And the more I worked with other bereaved parents, the more I realized that although everyone's story is different, so many aspects of the journey are shared, and people can take great comfort in knowing their experiences are not unique. The chapters that follow stem from many years of working with other bereaved parents, and recognizing the common things we all share.

The Journey of Grief

Our society does not deal well with grief. Often when people have suffered a loss, they are given a few weeks of close support, getting them through the funeral and a short time after. Then society expects them to be fine and get back to life. But grief doesn't respond to society's time line and schedule. Often grieving people are left feeling alone, guilty that they are not "getting it together" or that they are not strong enough, since they still feel all these difficult emotions. Adding to that feeling is having to try and sort it all out by themselves, without any knowledge of what is normal.

While we tend to think of grief in term of death, grief is a natural and normal reaction to any kind of loss. Death is the most obvious example, but a job change, a move, or a break-up in a relationship can all cause a similar kind of reaction. The term "grief" is used to describe that reaction. The word "bereavement" means to have suffered a loss, and "mourning" is the term used to describe the way people express their grief.

Grief is a process that encompasses many stages:

Postponement

The first stage of grief has traditionally been referred to as denial, but as anyone who has lived through it will agree, there is no denying what has happened. This stage is one of disbelief and follows the initial learning of the loss. Most often it is felt as emotional numbness or "shock." This is nature's way of making us go on autopilot for the first few days or weeks after a loss, allowing us to get through those first horrible days and all that needs to be done in funeral preparations and phone calls. Others will sometimes say a grieving person is "so strong" or "handling this all so well." I heard that from quite a few people after Nicholas died. "You are such a strong person! I don't think I could get through that." What else am I supposed to do, I would think.

At the same time, grieving people may feel as if they can't

think clearly, as if they are in a fog. This is usually the phase in which we receive the most support. People call, offer to bring meals, ask how we are doing. It is assumed that the person is in an active phase of grieving and needs support. In reality, however, the person is still feeling numb, unable to really begin to process all the emotional factors that are yet to come. When asked, they will answer that they can't think of anything someone else can do to help. Time seemed suspended to me. After my parents left and we were on our own for the first time since Nicholas died, I found myself feeling as if I had been caught in a time warp. I made a comment to a friend, wondering how long the intense pain of Nicholas' death would last, and she gently reminded me, "It's only been few days." I realized she was right. It had been only a week since we buried him, though it felt like weeks had passed. I wondered how long my life would seem to be happening in an alternate universe. This stage, unfortunately, often wears off at the point at which society expects people to begin to adjust and move on.

Anger

Anger is a very strong emotion and a part of every grief process. It can be directed at your spouse, kids, other pregnant women, other drivers on the highway, God, or even your unborn baby. You may find yourself snapping at your children or your spouse and later thinking "I blew that way out of proportion! What is wrong with me?" You may find yourself angry at a friend who is experiencing a normal pregnancy—why her and not me? You might find yourself angry at God for allowing such a thing to happen to you. It may even come out at your unborn baby: "How could you leave me like this?"

Anger can also surface in other ways:

Irritability: Instead of anger, you might feel grouchy,

edgy, or out of sorts. You may find you have no patience for things, however small. Little things your kids do may have you yelling at them. I remember losing my patience with Matthew almost daily after Victoria died. Three year old boys can drive a normally patient adult to distraction with pushing limits and being defiant, and Matthew was no exception. Even though, with my child psychology background, I knew that the behaviors were normal for his age, I had no patience with which to deal with them. And I felt awful afterwards for angrily sending him to time out instead of calmly correcting his transgressions. I found myself snapping at Aaron, also, about stupid things like leaving the cap off the toothpaste or not pulling the covers up on his side of the bed in the morning. Must I do everything around here?

Irritability may surface outside of your family as well. Stupid things other drivers do may make you shake your fists instead of shaking your head. You may feel burdened by previous commitments that now seem trivial. Why on earth did I say I'd bring cookies to the bake sale? Is my contribution really going to raise that much extra money?

Anxiety/Guilt: Grieving people often think "if only I had/ had not..., perhaps things might have been different." A feeling of guilt is actually anger turned inward on yourself. There were many days after Nicholas died when I thought, what if I hadn't gone to tea that day? Would he still be alive if I had been more careful about eating in restaurants? I knew I shouldn't blame myself, that eating something that would make us both sick was not an action I could have anticipated. And yet, I also knew it was a choice I had made, to eat that scone, that had led directly to his death. I would have jumped at the chance to go back in time and do things differently.

This is especially true for a woman who has had an unexplained miscarriage. "If only I hadn't lifted that box," "I never should have had that glass of wine." The "what if" game can drive you crazy. What if I had done things differently? What if we hadn't gone out, if I had gotten more sleep, if I hadn't eaten that spicy meal? Would things be better now?

Despite the fact that, in most cases, there is no reason to connect an outside action to a miscarriage, many women will tell themselves things might have been different "if only," looking for answers where there aren't any. If the pregnancy was not planned or if the parent was feeling ambivalent about this big change, they may think that their lack of excitement in some way contributed to the loss. It is important to remember that this is not your fault!

All these aspects of grief are normal. Anger must come out, or it will do more damage in the long run. However, we need to be careful at whom it is directed. Kids won't understand why you are yelling at them over little things. Your spouse is going through his or her own version of this process, and angry arguments can erupt over little things. When you find yourself snapping at your family or friends, step back and ask yourself whether you are really angry at this person or it is coming from somewhere else. Then say to that person, "I'm sorry, I'm having a really hard time right now. I didn't mean to take it out on you." Admitting to others that you are struggling with tough emotions will go a long way toward preventing damage to relationships. Looking back, I know I should have apologized more to my boys for being irritable and snapping at them, and I regret not doing that. But we also need to remember that we are only human, and we do the best we can with each day and each situation we are given. If you do let the anger come out at someone else, try to ask forgiveness, but also cut yourself some slack. You are coping with some pretty big emotions right now.

Depression

One of the strongest emotions in the grief process is sadness or depression. Emptiness and solitude are also strong aspects of this stage. Grieving people often say they feel hollow inside, as if a part of them is missing. For a woman who has lost a baby, these feelings can be physical, as well, especially if she had been able to feel the baby move.

There is often a need to be alone with one's feelings and thoughts, and that is okay, and even necessary as a part of this process. It's okay to turn down party invitations if you don't feel like being around other people. However, the need for solitude should not translate into isolating yourself from everyone or everything around you. Getting involved with an activity you enjoy, even if it seems to take a lot of extra effort, can keep you connected and keep the isolation from building to unhealthy levels. That was one of the reasons we turned to the theater for refuge. Getting involved with a show gave us both something to be doing that was outside of ourselves. I still had plenty of time to be alone with my feelings during the day when I was home by myself, but getting out to rehearsals every night kept me from sliding too far down into the sadness, for I had to interact with others and focus on what we were doing on the stage.

Depression can range from feelings of acute emotional pain accompanied by crying to a general feeling of melancholy or "feeling blue." Sadness can hang over everything you do during the day, always there but not preventing you from doing things, or be totally all consuming and preventing you from doing anything. It can intrude on your thoughts while you are focusing on something else. It can sap your energy and make you feel tired and listless. It can hang over your head and make you feel as if the sun will never shine on you again. Rest assured, despite the cliché sound of the words, time does heal the wounds. You will begin to smile and laugh again, and you will find over time that the ache in your chest will lessen. Remember that you are not being "disloyal" to your baby if you laugh and begin to enjoy your life again!

Healing

This final stage is usually referred to as acceptance or recovery, but many bereaved parents have difficulty with accepting what has happened. "Don't ask me to accept this—I'll never recover from it!" is a common statement. The term healing emphasizes that grieving is a journey, a process that may never feel fully complete.

This part of the process comes gradually and takes different amounts of time for different people. Sometimes people will say "I accepted this right away." They may mean that they are not pretending it didn't happen. Or, for them, perhaps the grief process moved quickly. Others may take years to get to the point of being able to move forward with their lives. One friend of mine had a cloud of sadness hanging over her for almost five years after multiple miscarriages. It began to seem, even to her closest friends, that she was unable to move forward with her life. For her, the journey took a long time—the important thing for the rest of us was to accept that she had to move with it at her own pace. Eventually, she did begin to find joy in her life again.

Acceptance comes from dealing with your feelings, doing the work that is involved in going through them, and coming to the point where you are "at peace" with what happened. This doesn't mean you will never think of it again. It doesn't mean you won't have moments in the future of tears or aches or longing. Even now, several years later, tears still come to my eyes when we visit Nicholas' grave. But acceptance does mean picking up the pieces, finding a new sense of normal, and moving forward with your life.

Grief is a very personal thing. While all human beings will share aspects of the process of grieving, no one can tell you how long it should take or what you should be feeling. Grief takes work, and it is hard to face the strong emotions it elicits. But if it is ignored or pushed aside, it will come back in some form later in life. It is much better to work through the process at the time.

The journey of grief is not a linear one. You will not move through one stage, check it off and be done with it, and then move on to the next. People often are surprised or shocked when they find themselves feeling an emotion they thought was gone weeks before. Grief is a "spiral" process, that moves from numbness to acceptance. A person will move through all these stages over and over again, sometimes feeling aspects of more than one stage at a time (anger and sadness, for instance), sometimes going long periods between the various emotions. You may think it is all behind you and then suddenly find yourself back in the middle of it again, thinking you will never get out.

Milestone dates may bring things back to the surface with surprising strength. The baby's due date fills many women with a strong sense of grief, even when they have been feeling more balanced in recent months. Some may find themselves feeling sad and not realizing why until late in the day. The baby's birth/death date will often have you reliving that horrible day over again in your head. I now tell women what Chris told me at Camp Trinity all those years ago: "Don't be alone on your due date." Or the anniversary date, as both of those can bring strong emotions to the surface.

The important thing to note is that over time, each of these passes through each stage of the grief process should be shorter and less intense. The spiral should go up, not down. Over time, the emotional pain should lessen to an ache. The times of solitude should not become isolation where you refuse to be around others. The times of sadness should not become bitterness or resentment. And eventually, you should come to a state of peace about your experience—not that it was okay that it happened, but that you have accepted that it happened and started moving on with your life.

If you find yourself in a spiral that goes downwards into deep sadness and despair, isolation or bitterness, not upwards back into life, it is time to seek help!

Grief Differences

Women often complain that their husbands don't seem to be upset by the loss of the baby. "I never see him cry." "Why isn't he hurting like I am?" "I don't think he loved our baby." are all common comments.

It is important to remember that men grieve differently from women. Women tend to talk to others about how they are feeling and what they are experiencing. They will share their stories of loss with others, and they will cry in the presence of friends. Men don't tend to show their emotions as much. Some may be trying to be strong for their wives; some may not think it manly. After Nicholas' burial, I was struck by the tears streaming down my husband's face at the cemetery. Later, I told him how much it had meant to me to see him cry, to know how much he was hurting, because he had never cried with the others.

"Yes, I did," he said. "I just did it in the shower. You never saw it."

What a comfort it would have been to me to have known that at the time! Just knowing that he was feeling a strong sense of loss, even if I never saw the tears, would have gone a long way in bridging the gap that I felt between us after Joshua and Victoria died. It had made me feel I was even more of a mess, when he seemed to be over it and moving on so quickly.

I think in some ways it is easier for men to get back to "normal" life. They go back to work and focus on their jobs, and at least while they are at work, can put it out of their minds. After the holidays, Aaron went back to work and focused on his projects and resumed his regular schedule. For me, however, motherhood is my job. There was no way to separate myself the way Aaron could, nothing to distract me during the day.

Men also don't let personal feelings show at work as often as women. Very few of Aaron's colleagues at work knew about Nicholas. I think he told a few of the guys with whom he worked most closely why he was out of the office, but most of the people with whom he worked never knew. I found it hurtful that he didn't tell more people at work. To me, it seemed that he cared less, though I knew that wasn't the case. I thought it was important for people to know about Nicholas, that somehow it validated his existence. And how could you not tell the people with whom you spend your whole day what was happening in your life? There was no way I could have kept it from people if I had wanted to—it was written all over my body language that something was terribly wrong. But for Aaron, the people at work were not close enough friends with whom to share that kind of intimate information. For him, sharing Nicholas was only for the closest inner circle.

Whether men show their feelings or not, grief will come out in some way. I have a friend whose husband would get involved in major house projects each time they lost a baby. He would build bookcases, replace floors, and engage himself in the "to do" list. At first, she was very angry that he wasn't upset about their losses. Then after a while, she began to see that working with tools was how he dealt with his grief. Physical labor was the outlet for him, the way that he worked through his feelings. Once she realized that, she was able to let him work through things his own way.

It is the men who don't seem to have any outlet about whom wives get very concerned. Another friend of mine commented to me that she was very worried about her husband after their babies died, for he seemed to feel he needed to be strong for her, and he never let anything show at all. She wanted him to break down and cry, not for her but for himself. She was afraid he was keeping it all inside, without an outlet, and it would be harmful to him both physically and emotionally in the long run.

The fact that men and women deal with the grief process very differently can cause great stress in a relationship—she wants him to talk with her, cry with her, show her that he feels what she does. He wants her to stop talking about it, for he deals with his feelings differently. Try to be supportive of each other and different approaches to grief. It is important to stay connected with each other even though you are mired in your own grief journey. If connections are not well maintained, distance can form between people, and relationships can be damaged.

Grief in Children

In cultures where multi-generational families share dwellings or villages where people live closely with each other, children are exposed to death at early ages, as a natural part of life. However, in our society, sick or elderly people are often not cared for at home. For many children, this loss of a baby sibling may be their first experience with death.

Adults often assume, incorrectly, that young children are not affected by grief. After all, they don't know enough about the world to find loss in it, right? But children often feel grief quite deeply. They are going to deal with a loss in different ways at different ages.

Toddlers

Adults assume that children under a certain age are not affected by a loss. To some extent, that is true. Children under the age of two will not have an understanding of what has happened. They are not going to feel sad or shed tears. However, they will begin to pick up on the emotional states of the adults in the household. They may become more clingy or whine and act out more, as they sense that something is wrong with their world.

Preschoolers

Many parents tell me that they did not tell their 2-6 year-old-children about the miscarriage because they figured they would not understand. Preschoolers, however, are capable of understanding much more than adults usually give them credit for. We did not think that Ryan was paying attention during Nicholas' burial service, he seemed distracted by the world around him. However, during grace at dinner several weeks later, Ryan suddenly said, "And God bless Nicholas in his little box in his big box." Aaron and I looked at each other across the table with wide eyes—Ryan had gotten much more of what was happening than we had thought. Even to the point of understanding the small box that was placed in the steel outer box was what really contained his baby brother.

Children know when something is wrong with the grownups in their world. They can tell when Mommy or Daddy seems upset or worried. They also hear what grownups are saying—adults tend to forget that when kids seem to be off in their own world playing on the other side of the room, they can hear what is being said around them. They hear conversations on the phone, and they watch how people are behaving. When no explanation is given, they will often internalize it and think it has something to do with them or their behavior.

Kids tend to "take the blame" for things they don't understand, and they get scared when they feel that their world is out of control or not normal. It is better to be honest with them, when possible. If they already knew about the new baby, then they must be told that the baby has died. It is best not to say things like "went away" or "went to sleep," for those kinds of euphemisms can cause concern for the child that others might disappear or something might happen to him if he goes to sleep at night. If they did not know, tell them something like, "We were going to have a new baby in our house, but that baby has died and Mommy feels very sad right now." This will likely bring about matter-of-fact questions like "Why?" that will be hard to answer, but at least the child will be able to understand that something else is upsetting his parents, not him.

Don't expect emotional responses to the news that the baby had died, though some children may exhibit them. A young child will not deal with this news in the same way as you. And don't be offended by things your child says that you may find hurtful. "It's okay, Mom, we didn't need that baby anyway. You have me." Those are not things that are said to deliberately hurt you, but they reflect the way children deal with their world. Ryan told people who came to our house that "our baby died." He didn't seem sad about it. After all, he did not know what it meant to have a new baby in the house, so he had no emotional attachment the way the rest of us did. He did spend time in the following weeks trying to get answers to his questions, which no one seemed to be able to answer adequately for him. He polled many adults over the holidays, asking, "Why did the baby die?" As painful as that question was to hear over and over, it was his way of trying to make sense out of an event that had caused his normal life to become very confused.

Sometimes the processing of stressful events in their lives can be witnessed through a child's play. You may see them reenacting phone conversations or memorial services with dolls or stuffed animals. They may tell their animals stories about the baby or about a mommy who is sad. Young children have a very difficult time expressing emotions, and play is often a way they work through new or different experiences. There are also several good books for children about losing a baby sibling, which can help a child talk about and process what is happening in his/her family (see reference section at the back of this book for titles).

School-Age Children

School-age children have a better idea of what dying means. They understand that it is final, that the person is not coming back. Many of them have had a friend whose pet has died or who have lost a grandparent. This age is more likely to have an emotional reaction to the news that the baby is gone. There may be tears or sadness or a repeated wish that "the baby didn't have to die."

Children this age also have a better sense of what it would

have meant to have a new baby in the house—though their feelings about having it happen in their own family might have been conflicted. If they were not pleased about having a new baby, they may feel guilty that they somehow caused the baby to die. They may also feel angry that this is taking their parents' attention away from them or be afraid that something might happen to someone else in the family.

Children experience a wide range of emotions at this age, but they often have a hard time expressing them in words. They may be unable to express that they are afraid something will happen to Mommy now, too. You may see the grief on the surface at first; then they will "go back to normal" but begin having trouble sleeping at night. They may begin acting out or showing a regression of behavior as a way to get Mommy or Daddy's full attention again.

You might find them needing more physical contact, hugs, and snuggles than they did, and not just from family. It is a good idea to alert other adults such as a teacher or day care provider, with whom your child spends long periods of time, what is happening at home, so that they are prepared for questions or unusual behaviors should they arise. Matthew's first grade teacher found he seemed to need to sit on her lap at points during the school day, something she was knew was connected to Nicholas' death.

The best way to handle behavior changes is to give the children lots of love and reassurance. Make sure they know that their parents are not going to go away and that the grownups will be feeling better soon. If you are having a bad day and feeling an emotional mess, be honest with them. Tell them "Mommy's feeling very sad today." Apologize to them if you snap at them, and let them know it is not their fault. That is one thing I don't think I did enough. I know there were plenty of times when I snapped at my boys over some small thing and felt like a heel for it later. It is very difficult to have the strength to emotionally support someone else when you feel so low yourself.

So how do you help your kids through their journey when your own emotional state is such a wreck? You do the best you can, and cut yourself a lot of slack. You will not be a basket case forever, and your kids will forgive your shortcomings.

It is important to remember that people deal with grief in their own way. Some women don't seem affected by a miscarriage, and perhaps they truly do not feel an intense sense of loss. Or perhaps they are private people who do not like to show their inner selves to others. Some people need to talk about their situations over and over again; others need to hide away from the world and sift through their feelings alone. For some, the sadness hangs over them like a cloud, not for weeks or months but for years.

Grief is a journey, one that has a beginning, a middle, and an end. It may take months or even years to make it all the way through the middle and begin to see an end. The end of the grief process does not mean you love your baby any less or that you have forgotten or "gotten over" the loss at all. It means you are moving on with your life and continuing to live, which is important. No, life will not return to the "normal" you once had. You have been changed by this experience, and your life will never be exactly as it was. Your heart will always bear the scars—but they won't always hurt. Life will take on a new sense of normal, and you will find beauty and joy in things again.

Am I Going Crazy?

There are definitely points during the grief process when you will feel as if you are losing your mind. If you don't have friends or family who have been through a similar experience, expressing those fears may be difficult, as others may not understand they are real. They might even try to brush them aside by saying, "Oh, you're being silly. Of course you are not going crazy!" Included in this section are some of the things I have heard women admit to feeling.

"I still feel the baby move."

A friend of mine was talking to me a month or so after losing her twins at 21 weeks and hesitantly said, "This is going to sound crazy, but I still feel them moving." That doesn't sound crazy at all, I told her. I had the same experience after Nicholas died. It's awful. She sounded so relieved to know someone else had experienced this same thing. Rather like an amputee who says a lost leg itches, feeling a lost baby moving is a cruel trick the mind or nature plays. Muscles twitching, air bubbles, who knows what is really happening biologically. Whatever the cause, it is most unfair. And it is a very common complaint among women who have lost a baby after movement was felt—if they are in an environment where they are comfortable admitting they experience it. Most often when it comes up in a group discussion, there is obvious relief in knowing "I'm not going crazy."

"I cry at TV commercials/songs on the radio."

After Nicholas died, it seemed to me that every time I turned on the radio, Amy Grant's "Baby, Baby" was playing. I would immediately turn off the radio. I love Amy Grant's music, but that song would stab my heart each time I heard it. Why? This song is all about the joys of motherhood and being "here for you always and forever." Except that my baby wasn't here.

Whether we are going through a good experience or a bad

one, there will always be things on TV or the radio that remind you of what you are experiencing. If it is a happy thing, then each reminder only adds to that happiness. But when it is something difficult or sad, each reminder adds to the pain. Further along in "Baby, Baby" is the line "Ever since the day you put my heart in motion, baby I realize that there's no getting over you." That's the truth, I would think—I don't think I'll ever get over this.

I was amazed at how many songs on the radio had to do with turning back time and changing the course of events. Even the Backstreet Boys sing about it: "Sometimes I wish I could turn back time, impossible as it may seem. But I wish I could so bad..." Every time I would hear that song, I would think back to the day I met my friends for tea. What if I could go back and change that one moment in time? Would Nicholas still be alive? Of course, there is no way to know. And now, I can't say I would go back and change it, for then Tristan would not be here. But in the months following Nicholas' death, those songs would make my heart break every time I heard them.

You can either avoid such things by turning off the radio or TV when you react to something you are hearing, or you can let the emotions come on as strong as they need to and indulge in a good cry. Protection of your emotions or purging of them; there are advantages to both tactics. Depending on where you are in the grieving process, you might choose differently on different occasions. But reacting to things like songs does not mean anything except that you are in tune with your emotional state, and it is in a fragile place.

"I get depressed each time I get my period."

Biologically, the hormone shifts associated with a loss and then returning to regularity can cause the first cycle or two to be unusually heavy, bringing the experience of the loss vividly back to the surface again. The first cycle after the loss of a baby can be almost as bad as the experience itself. It is a fresh reminder of what is no longer there. It is also a signal that your body has gone on and is "back to normal," ready to do the whole thing all over again. That often coincides with emotionally beginning to really try to process what happened, and it can feel like a betrayal to have your body saying "I'm ready." How can my body forget so quickly what it used to be doing?

As the months go by, the return of each month's cycle can be either a source of frustration, if you are trying to conceive again, or a beginning of a looking forward as you think about the possibilities. Some women who want to get pregnant again and then have trouble conceiving become depressed each month that they don't have the baby they so long to hold. Like those who struggle with infertility, that monthly reminder can make the longing worse. Others who want to give themselves more time might start to look at each month and think ahead to what might be.

"Every woman in the world seems pregnant."

It probably seems that suddenly every woman you meet is pregnant—I certainly felt that way after losing both Victoria and Nicholas. Close friends seemed to be announcing pregnancies every other day. Chances are you are simply much more aware of pregnant women than you used to be. It is kind of like when a child trying to wheedle her mom into buying something tells her that "everyone else has one." Chances are she is not the only one in the world without said item, but she could only focus on the ones around her who were part of the special group she longed to join. Your senses are more "tuned in" to protruding bellies because you are so aware of your own body and desires.

"Why are other people's prayers answered and not mine?"

This is a question for which there are no answers. Sometimes it does feel, even to people of strong faith, that God is singling them out only to ignore their pleas. Particularly if many of your friends are having babies, it may seem that everyone else's prayers are being answered but yours. How you work through this challenge is purely an individual thing. Everyone's spiritual lives are their own journeys.

Many people find their faith shaken by the death of a baby —mine certainly was following Nicholas' death. These kind of life experiences can either drive someone away from her faith, or strengthen it. Clergy and other pastoral counselors can aid in that journey, but this is one area where it is really between you and God to work out the answer.

"No one seems to understand—they all think I'm "dwelling" too much."

Unless someone has been through a miscarriage herself, there is no way to fully understand what you are feeling. Just as I have no way of fully understanding what life is like for my friend who has a handicapped child, so only those who have experienced this same kind of loss can truly understand what you are going through. There will be friends who are incredibly supportive without having experienced this kind of a loss themselves, and there will be friends who will tell you to just get pregnant again and get over it already. Hopefully, there will be more of the former than the latter, but not always. After Nicholas died, my friend Liz would listen to me talk about him and justify my feelings without ever having experienced a loss herself. She felt she couldn't be of help to me because of that—she told me over and over how she couldn't begin to imagine what I was feeling. But she let me talk and supported the time the grief process takes, without judgment.

Many women tell me that they have one special friend who will listen to them talk over and over again while their own mother or sister gets fed up with hearing about the loss. Support can come from unexpected places. If you have no one around you who has had a similar experience, search in your area for a support group for infant loss. Many hospitals offer support services. There are also dozens of pregnancy loss websites, many of which have chat rooms or online support groups. You will be amazed to find how many people out there do understand.

"Holidays are so hard."

Many women find holidays to be particularly difficult after the death of a baby. Gatherings of friends and family, often with lots of children running around, can make even the 4th of July hard on someone grieving a loss. However, some holidays are more difficult than others.

Mother's Day: The second Sunday in May is set aside for honoring our mothers and giving them special attention and treatment. We buy corsages and take our mothers out to brunch. Kids take great pride in making secret projects to bestow upon Mom in bed Sunday morning.

I think this is one of the hardest holidays for women who have lost a child, especially if they have no other living children. Most churches offer a special blessing for mothers on Mother's Day—but what of the woman who has no living children? Most will say it is hard for them to watch this blessing and not be included, but they also feel it is too hard to stand up with other mothers when their children are no longer there. One of my friends won't even go to church on Mother's Day, she finds it so hard that her four non living children don't count towards her being recognized as a mother.

The prominence of Mother's Day cards and gifts in our society makes it difficult to get away from it. For women who have lost a child, it is a painful reminder of what isn't there. Father's Day can be equally difficult for the men. On both these holidays, the roles of mother and father go unrecognized for those whose babies have died.

Christmas/Thanksgiving: Many people find these two holidays to be particularly difficult because of large family gatherings that take place during this time of year. Many parents feel the hole in the gathering where their child should be, and yet the rest of the family does not seem to recognize or mention the missing child. It can be extra difficult for those who have no living children to be surrounded by nieces and nephews. Christmas, in particular, is difficult, for the excitement of the children and the attention they get from the rest of the family only add to the bereaved parents' feelings of loss.

"I don't think I'll ever get over the fear of this happening again!"

So many times women have asked me, "How do you get over the fear?" The reality is, you don't get over it, not fully anyway. In addition to robbing you of your baby, miscarriage robs you of ever having a carefree pregnancy in the future. Most women who experience a miscarriage go on to have another healthy, full-term pregnancy, but there is still anxiety involved for most of them. Even when you feel really ready to have another baby, there will probably still be days when you struggle with fear, especially until you pass the time of the previous loss. Ryan, Tristan and Griffin's pregnancies were all filled with days of anxiety, even as every indications pointed to a healthy, normal pregnancy. There were many days I felt like I was waiting for the proverbial shoe to fall.

How do you handle those days of anxiety? Particularly in the first trimester, there is little you can do or see to help reduce that fear. You can try prayer, meditation, yoga—whatever works to help you relax. And sometimes, you just have to ride it out. If you need to have ten minutes of panic, give yourself the ten minutes. But try not to let the ten minutes turn into all day, for that kind of anxiety isn't good for you (or the baby). I knew I was never going to completely relax with Tristan or Griffin's pregnancies until they were safely in my arms. But I tried to put as much trust into each day as I could. And no, it was not easy. The important thing is not to let the fear keep you from going ahead with what you want to do.

"When am I going to get over this?"

How long it takes to get "back to normal" or "get over" a pregnancy loss is a personal thing. Some women may "get over" it quickly and move on with life. Others will tell you that they will never fully get over the loss of a child, and this experience will always be a part of who they are. The reality is that you are a different person from who you were before this loss, and your life is different now, in a small way or a large one.

People move through this grief process at their own pace, and no one around them should tell them how quickly it should be happening. It may be weeks, it may be a year or more, but eventually, you should find yourself feeling better, enjoying life's activities, and finding your world looking cheerful rather than dark. However, if it seems to you, or to those around you, that this is not happening in a reasonable amount of time, it is time to seek some professional guidance and support.

"When will the anniversaries get easier?"

The first time we approached Nicholas' due date and birthday were definitely the most difficult. The emotional pain of those dates was almost as strong as the weeks following his death. In the years since, it has gotten easier. I no longer feel those emotions as strongly, and yet, I am very aware of the the significance of the day. I have a little pin of tiny footprints that I wear on the anniversaries (and on Mother's Day), to remember Nicholas. If people ask, I tell them why I am wearing it. If they don't, he is still closer to my heart throughout the day. Those days can also feel very lonely, if no one else remembers what day it is. I have one friend who always sends me an email on Nicholas' birthday—as I do on her twins' birthday—just to let me know someone else remembers him. I am always grateful for her acknowledgment, for it is comforting to know that someone else is thinking of him that day.

You may also find yourself struck by the milestones in years to come. I remember being very aware of the day that Nicholas would have started kindergarten. Was it a day of tears and sorrow? No. But I was aware of the milestone that he was missing. As we walked into the building for Matthew's high school graduation, I was suddenly struck by the thought that we should be celebrating two sons that day. Zachary should also have been graduating. Did that realization diminish the celebratory mood of the day and leave me feeling sad? No. But I took comfort from the gentle squeeze of Aaron's hand and allowed myself a few minutes of feeling wistful at what we were missing.

The anniversaries are hard, no question about it. However, they should get easier over time. Mark those days in a special way: wear a special piece of jewelry, attend a religious service, light a candle, have a birthday cake—whatever helps you to feel connected to your baby.

"What do I say when people ask how many children I have?"

This is a tough one for many women, particularly if the

baby died later in the pregnancy. I still have a hard time answering this question. One man I know responded without hesitation that he had seven, counting his three in heaven. If people continued the conversation, he would tell them about the ones who are missing from the family. I have a hard time saying all that to people I don't know well, but I admire his ability to do it without hesitation.

I always feel bad if I don't "count" my four non-living children, as if they aren't worthy of mentioning. But do I really need to go into all this each time someone asks me this question? Most of the time, I just say "four" and add the others silently in my head. Sometimes I tell people I have four growing sons, knowing that does not discount the four who are not growing on this Earth. Sometimes, though, I reply that I have four living children, if the situation is one where I don't mind going into more details. But it can be a conversation stopper, as well, so it's a fine line to walk.

Another question that was hard for me was "Is this your first?" For me, it was most difficult when I was pregnant with Tristan, the year after Nicholas died. I couldn't honestly say this was my third, but I also didn't want to go into Nicholas' story each time, either. I usually just replied that I had an eight year old and a four year old and left it at that. But it never felt quite right.

If you have no living children, the question of "do you have kids?" is a painful one. Yes, I have them, but they are not here. Most women just say no, though it pains them to do so—but does this person you've just met really need to hear your life story? The answer to any of these questions has to be based upon what you feel comfortable sharing. Remember that you are not being disloyal to your baby if you choose not to go into it each time the question comes up!

Most of the time, people are unaware of your situation and don't mean to say things to hurt you, but that doesn't change how you feel each time you have to face the question. I had occasion to be at a function with a woman with whom I had a slight acquaintance, whom I had not seen since before her second child was born. Our oldest sons were the same age, and she promptly asked me in a room full of people, "So, when are you going to have another one?" My friends in the room stiffened, for we had just gone through the second miscarriage two months before. The question hurt, but I felt I had no choice but to answer it. It also made me angry—how dare you ask me something so personal in a room full of people I don't know? Although I knew she had no way of knowing my situation, I looked at her pointedly and replied, "Actually, we just recently lost two." She had no idea what to say to me, and the room had a rather awkward silence for a minute, but I thought, perhaps you'll think before you come out with such things in the future, for you never know someone else's story.

Remember this: you are not going crazy. You are going through a very difficult experience. Life has handed you one of the worst experiences you could imagine ever happening, and it takes time to work through it. But you are not losing your mind. Grief is a very individual thing, and while we share common feelings, everyone deals with them differently. Reacting to a difficult experience by avoiding things that add to the pain or hearing things that seem to make it worse are normal parts of protecting your fragile emotional state while you focus on healing.

There will be days when you feel as if you have it all together and are past the worst of the pain, and the next day you might feel your heart is raw and bleeding all over again. If you are having a bad day, allow yourself to have it. Being where you are in the process and giving yourself permission to let emotions ebb and flow as they need to do will ease the journey in the long run. However, if you don't see a change in how you react to certain songs or other pregnant women over time, or if you don't see the pain beginning to lessen in reaction, then you might need to think about seeking help to work through your grief. Needing help doesn't mean that you are not strong enough to handle things on your own. But you need to be able to resume your life, whatever new sense of normal you find for it.

*Hurtful Things Well
Meaning People Say*

In a perfect world, people would receive the kind of support they need from those around them at all times. However, the reality is, you will have to deal with people saying things you find hurtful, whether they mean it or not. You probably have already experienced someone saying something you found to be hurtful and not helpful. People who have been through this experience themselves usually will offer a hug, an "I'm so sorry," or a listening ear. But those who haven't experienced this kind of loss often don't know what to say. So they say something, hoping to make you feel better and, in fact, they do the opposite. These are some of the most common comments women find to be hurtful:

"It is all for the best. Something must have been wrong."/ "Everything happens for a reason."

When you consider all the thousands of things that have to be just right in order to have a healthy, full-term baby, it is easier to understand why so many women experience a miscarriage. Medically, in many cases, miscarriages are nature's way of taking care of a fetus that is not growing properly. In Joshua's case, something was most likely wrong from the start, which is why the test never registered as positive. But that did not change the ache in my heart one bit. So, while this statement may be true, it doesn't make me feel better.

"I understand how you feel."

It always made me angry to hear people say they knew how I felt when they had not experienced this trauma. Unless the speaker has been through a loss of this kind her/himself, they do not understand how you feel. They might be able to imagine how they would feel in the same situation, they might have gone through grief themselves and be able to empathize with you. But unless someone has experienced the loss of a baby, they don't understand how you feel.

"You are young. You can always have another."

This statement can be hurtful in more than one way. For many people, the "can always have another" isn't true. I know too many women who had multiple losses and were never able to have a successful pregnancy. But more importantly, it glosses over the fact that this child is gone. Saying "You can have another" makes it sound as if this baby is easily replaceable, like a burned-out light bulb. Most women I have talked to think, "But I wanted this baby. Even if I do go on to have another baby someday, it won't replace this one." A subsequent child will help to fill the hole, but can never be a replacement. When people say "You can always have another," it makes light of the bond that has already formed between mother and child.

"Don't worry, you'll be pregnant again soon."

Here again, a well meaning person makes what amounts to a flippant remark, making the mother feel that what happened really isn't that important. It disregards her feelings and makes the baby sound easily replaceable. A subsequent pregnancy will not replace the baby who has died. That baby mattered and was loved for herself, no matter what her gestational age.

"At least it happened early—it's not as though you lost a real child."

When a child dies after birth, regardless of the age of the child, society sees it as a tragedy and extends comfort to the family. After all, that child had a place in the family, a seat at the dinner table, a car seat in the van. But when a baby dies in the early stages of development, people don't see things the same way. After all, no one could see this child. We didn't know his/her name or often even its gender. Maybe the mother never felt it move. So how could there be a bond already there? Why should we mourn something that wasn't really a person?

Many people look at a miscarriage as having lost a pregnancy, not a living baby. But that heart was beating and now has stopped. This little person was real, was unique, and was loved whether anyone could see it or not.

"Be thankful for the child/ren you already have."/ "Having a child already must be such a comfort to you."

I think many people assume that if you already have a child, then losing a baby doesn't hurt as much. After all, your living child must be a comfort for you. And that is true, to some degree. However, just because I already have a child doesn't mean that this child who is gone was wanted or loved any less. Having a child already doesn't take the place of the one that is gone, or ease the ache from that loss. And having children to care for means you don't get the time to heal physically and emotionally following a loss—you are forced to get back into life.

On the other hand, you are forced to get back into life and at least go through the motions of each day. Believe me, I was very thankful to have children in my home already. How much worse it was for my friends who had lost their first child and had no one to help them get back to life again. Matthew and Ryan kept me going in the weeks following Nicholas' death. There were plenty of days when all I wanted to do was crawl under the covers and hide from the world—the world didn't understand how much my heart was hurting, after all. But I couldn't do that. I had two little boys who needed me. And as hard as it was to care for them and feel I was doing a good job at it, they forced me to get out of bed and continue living. So yes, I thank God for my children each day. But that doesn't change the fact that there are four other children I still miss.

"I can't begin to imagine your pain."

This sounds like a nice thing to say to someone, since no

one can ever understand what another person is feeling at the time of a tragedy. However, one bereaved mother I met told me that this was the worst comment for her to hear. It made her feel as if her experience was so awful, so unique, no one could understand it. Although she realized this person was trying to say they weren't going to pretend they could understand what she was feeling, it also made her feel as if she was so far out there that no one could even try to reach her. It left her feeling more alone than ever.

"Are you going to try again?"

I hate the phrase "try again." To me, it implies that I failed at something. But I didn't fail at anything. My baby died—there is a big difference. "Try again" makes it seem like an opportunity was lost, not a member of my family, and so invalidates the baby. The question also makes it sound as if success is dependent on trying hard enough. If you want to have a baby badly enough, just keep trying and eventually you will succeed. But that is so often not the case. I began using the term "have another" when people asked. For I had this baby, however briefly.

When Tristan was little, people who saw we had three boys would often ask, "Are you going to have another one, and try for a girl?" If we were to have another child, I would think, it would be because we wanted another child and not because we wanted a girl child. But it wasn't a question I could answer yet.

After Nicholas died, I felt very strongly that our family was not complete. But after Tristan was born, I didn't know. There was a part of me that said this has just been too hard—I have three beautiful kids, and don't need to put myself through this any more. But I didn't have a strong sense of completion either. It was not a decision to be made lightly. I had never had two consecutive pregnancies be successful and, even though Donna would tell me that has no bearing on a subsequent pregnancy, it is a hard fact to push aside,

206

emotionally. Any decision to have another child would have to be well thought through—or an unexpected gift.

And that is exactly what Griffin is. We were passed the point of making a conscious choice to have another child. I had reached the point of being content with raising my three boys and snuggling other people's babies. Would I have been able to say "I want to do this again" and make a decision to have another baby? At this point, I don't know. I doubt it. The journey had been too difficult and the risks too great for me to decide to climb that mountain again. And yet, as difficult as the climb to the top was that final time, I tell often tell people, "God threw us for a loop, but He knew what he was doing."

"It was God's will."

I think this is the statement with which I have the most difficulty. I heard this from friends after Nicholas died, and it infuriated me. I know when people face a friend undergoing tragic circumstances about which no one can make sense, they often respond with a "will of God" philosophy because it takes tragic circumstances out of human control and relieves people of the burden of trying to make sense of a situation that has no explanation (like "Why did the baby have to die?"). But I have a very hard time believing in a God who would deliberately take my child away from me. That just doesn't mesh with my image of a loving God. I can deal better with medical science saying, "This is tragically unfair and never should anyone have to face this." It is much more difficult to imagine God saying, "I think I'll inflict this horrible pain on you just because I feel like it." I much prefer the image of a loving, caring God shedding tears with me and holding me close through my pain.

"God needed another angel in Heaven"

I never personally heard this comment, but I have friends who have. It is another way of saying it was "God's will," and

I have just as much trouble with this statement, for the same reasons. The thought that God would give me something and then say, "On second thought, I need that child more than you do" and take it back just doesn't mesh with my image of a loving God. I don't see God giving things and taking them back on a whim.

"God never gives you more than you can handle." /"When God closes a door, somewhere he opens a window."

I think this is a way of saying, "I know you are strong enough to get through this." And of course, it is true that every person will find a way to survive whatever tragedies are thrown at them in life, for what choice is there? However, I put these statements in the same category as "It was God's will." It implies that God chose to inflict this experience on me, singled me out for this horrible nightmare. Was He testing me to see exactly how much I could take without breaking? Or did He decide that I am stronger than someone else and could handle it better? I have a very difficult time accepting that my babies died in order to somehow make me a stronger person. I may be stronger as a result of these tragedies, but I can't believe that God deliberately inflicted them on me.

Silence

As hard as it is to hear these kinds of platitudes that really don't help, I think the worst is when people don't say anything at all. Silence can be just as hurtful, even more so, for it makes the parents feel isolated. At least the people who say the wrong things are acknowledging that you have had a difficult experience, even if they inadvertently say something hurtful. But the friends who are silent can make you feel as if what you are going through needs to be kept quiet and not talked about. Now, most of those folks are not trying to say that at all, and would be appalled that anyone mistook their silence for uncaring. Most of them would say one of the following things:

"I didn't know what to say to you."

There are no words that anyone can say, even those who have themselves been through it, that will make you feel suddenly better. The only thing that truly helps is time. There are three little words that do help, though: "I'm so sorry." Really, that is all we want to hear, right? "I'm sorry for your loss" validates what you are experiencing and lets you know they are thinking of you.

"I didn't want to make you feel bad/remind you by bringing it up."

This one always confuses me—as if mentioning the thing that is foremost in my thoughts right now is going to make me feel worse! Believe me, you are not going to be reminding me of something I've forgotten! Most of the women I have talked to needed to talk about their experience and their feelings. They needed to validate the importance of this short little life by hearing people acknowledge that it existed.

We got an incredible amount of support when Nicholas died—emails and phone calls came from friends far and wide. We had written about Nicholas in our Christmas letter, and we got notes from people we had not heard from in long time. And yet there were holes in the network, places where close friends remained silent, and we wondered why. I'm sure most of those people were hurting for us and just didn't know what to say. But the silence made me feel as if those people did not care about us any longer.

Sometimes, silence happens because of misunderstanding. After Nicholas died, I asked one of our friends to spread the word among our theater friends, for I did not want to have to go through the story over and over again, anymore than I already had to do. And yet, I wanted the people at the theater to know before the next time we went there. They all knew I was pregnant, and I couldn't deal with telling them all individually. So I left that up to the network to spread. I expected we would get calls and emails from at least some of them, and we did get a few emails. But mostly, there was nothing but silence. This only made us feel worse, as if no one cared.

It was only several months later, at the close of the Once Upon A Mattress, that our loss came up in conversation. We had gotten hugs and condolences when we came to our first rehearsal, but it wasn't until the end of the run of the show that I found out that in December word had gone out that we didn't want to talk to anyone about it. Somehow, the "I can't handle telling everyone" had become "they want to be left alone." All the time that we were at home feeling as if no one cared, our friends at the theater were thinking they were respecting our wishes by keeping their distance! When they found out about the misunderstanding, they felt awful and told us how many times we had been in conversation in the weeks that followed Nicholas' death. How much it would have meant to me at the time to know that! Though there was nothing that could be done to go back and fill that void, it did make us feel so much better knowing that the love was definitely there all along.

What is the best way to deal with people who say things you find hurtful? That is a personal decision. For the most part, I kept quiet and didn't say anything directly to the person, particularly if it came from a friend. I would stew about it in my head or rant about it to Aaron later, but I tended to refrain from responding to most of these statements.

However, there are times when I later felt that I should have said something and perhaps educate the person. Perhaps if I tell them how hurtful their comment was, they would think twice before saying it to someone else.

If you choose to respond, you should be careful how you do. Educating someone calmly and gently will encourage them to have a different view of your situation and how they speak to others. Yelling at them will probably make them think poorly of you and not allow what you say to carry over to other situations. In the same way ignoring or showing anger to someone for what they have said, without explaining why you are hurt by what they said, will only damage relationships.

It is important to remember that most of the people who say stupid things aren't trying to be mean. They honestly don't know what to say to bring comfort, so platitudes are all they can find. We've all been guilty of making the same mistakes to others, knowingly or not. If you don't feel it is worth risking otherwise good relationships, take care with how you respond.

Ways to Memorialize Your Baby

For those who have a baby die in the latter stages of pregnancy, there are ways to remember the baby that are not available to those who miscarry earlier. There is a graveside to visit, pictures, or a piece of hair, perhaps. But for those for whom the loss was early, there often isn't anything to hold on to later. Fortunately, there are ways to create a memorial or remember your baby:

Give your baby a name

Even if you never felt the baby move or have no idea if it was a boy or a girl, giving your child a name can be very healing. It allows you to refer to your baby as an individual and not just as an abstract concept or medical issue.

There are a number of ways you can look at choosing a name. If you don't know the gender of the baby, you can choose a "neutral" name that could be given to either a boy or a girl. Or you can go with the inner feeling of it having been one or the other—after all, if you are wrong, does it really matter? You can look at the meaning of names and choose something based on what its meaning says to you. Some people have a hard time with giving the baby a real name, and choose to go with something more abstract. For example, one woman I know had referred to the baby in utero as "Harpo," an affectionate little nickname for a child whose gender was unknown to them. When that child died in the second trimester, the parents couldn't bring themselves to change the name, so Harpo is how they continue to refer to the baby.

No one can tell you there is a right or a wrong way to go about creating a name for your child. Whatever feels right and comfortable to you is what you should do. Nor is there a time frame by which it must be done. It is never to late to give your child a name. I have a friend who named her son more than thirty years after he was stillborn. At the memorial masses we have had following the workshops, the name of each baby is read out loud while the family lights a candle. I always tell people that "Baby" and their last name is perfectly fine, for God knows this child. I have had the experience on multiple occasions of having someone come back to me after the mass and tell me they have finally given their child a name and to thank me for giving them the encouragement to do so. There can be healing in speaking a name, whenever you are ready to do it.

Plant a tree

Many people I know have planted a tree or a shrub or created a special little part of their garden in memory of their infant. We planted three azaleas under our bay window for Zachary, Victoria, and Joshua. And Nicholas' tree stands a few feet away in the front yard. Very few people know why those particular plants are there, but it makes me feel good to look at them and see a living, growing, blooming thing in memory of each of my little ones.

Write your baby a letter

For some people, writing can be therapeutic. Many people find they can put into words on paper what they cannot say to others in person. Writing to your baby can bring about a sense of connection. I kept a journal with each of my pregnancies, and for the last two, I wrote it in the form of letters to the baby. When Nicholas' pregnancy journal became one of loss, I continued to write to him, telling him how I was feeling and how much I missed him. Through addressing him in writing, I felt I was able to speak to him, that perhaps he was able to hear me somehow.

Keep a journal

Even if you can't bring yourself to write directly to your baby, keeping a journal can still be a good way of working through deep feelings. Sometimes it is easier to let those feelings spill out onto paper than to say them out loud. Get a pretty blank book or an inexpensive spiral notebook. No one else ever has to read it if you don't want to share it. You can write about how unfair this all is, how much your heart hurts, whatever it is you are feeling at that particular time. You can just scribble on the page until it is solid black if that helps. You may find that you are working through feelings you couldn't identify before, just by letting you hand write whatever comes into your head. Later, your journal might be something to read through as a memento or to burn as a symbol of letting go.

Light a candle

Many churches still have areas of candles you can light for a special intention. Or you can light a candle at home on your child's due date, birth/death date, or other special day of memory.

Attend a service

Having a memorial service for your baby can bring some closure to the loss. It can be a formal service at church (having a mass said, for instance), or it can be something you put together in your backyard. You can invite those who are close to you, or let it be private, just you and your partner. Read a poem, light a candle, sing a song, whatever helps you. After each of the workshops, we held a memorial mass for infants, where parents were invited to light a candle for each of their infants as the names are read out loud. At our hospital, the Labor and Delivery nurses hold a White Rose ceremony each spring, near Mother's Day, where bereaved families can come and share time in community with others. As part of a short memorial service, every family is invited to come tie a white ribbon on a tree in memory of their infant. In the December meeting of our Empty Arms support group, we have a candle lighting ceremony, for so many parents find the holidays to be very difficult. In many communities, services like this are held at local hospitals or through local support groups. Ask around and you may find a special event that happens every year.

Create a memory book

If your baby died later in the pregnancy or after birth, the hospital will likely provide you with items to keep, such as photographs, a lock of hair, a blanket, or a tee shirt. It is likely you will have cards and things to keep as well. All these things can be kept in a special box of some kind or mounted into a shadow box, or you can create a memory book from the paper items with larger items kept separately. None of these things need to be done right away—it's perfectly fine to put them away in a closet until you are able to face the emotions involved in assembling something.

It is harder to create a memory book if you lose a baby early in the pregnancy, but you could include copies of emails or cards from friends expressing their sorrow. Perhaps you had an ultrasound photo from an early exam. Whatever things you might have received, arranging them in a blank book or scrapbook of some kind can give you a tangible thing to keep as a memento. I made a memory book for Nicholas, with all the cards, printouts of emails, and photos of flowers that were sent. Although it still makes me very sad to look through it, it also reminds me of all the supportive people who were such a help to us during that time.

Purchase a keepsake

There are many websites that offer keepsakes in memory of miscarried babies. Jewelry, artwork, garden memorials, and Christmas ornaments are among the many kinds of keepsakes available. Some websites are listed in the resource section at the back of this book.

Ornament for the tree

Many people tell me that having a special ornament for

their Christmas tree or small statue on their shelf is of great comfort. I keep all four of our special angel ornaments packed together in one little box, and they always hang in the same area of our tree each year, all together. It makes me feel that those little souls are a more prominent part of our family during the holidays, when I can look at the tree and see my angels.

Create a memory/angel garden

Many people create a special place in their yard for a memorial to their child. It can include statues, plaques (these can be ordered on line), bushes, trees, whatever speaks to you and creates a place that is special to you. Another option is to create a special place of beauty that can be enjoyed by many people at your church or in a local park, with permission, of course. You can include a small statue or plaque naming the place in memory of your child, or it can just stand alone.

Angel of Hope

In, The Christmas Box, a worldwide bestseller by author Richard Paul Evans, a woman mourns the loss of her child at the base of an angel monument. Though the story is mostly fiction, a bronze statue was commissioned and installed in Salt Lake City by the author in response to reports that grieving parents were seeking out the angel as a place to grieve and heal. Across the nation, there are now many "Angel of Hope" gardens, created as a symbol of hope for all parents that grieve the death of a child. Each garden contains an angel statue, with the face of a child, and many of these gardens have an "adopt a brick" program, where you can purchase a brick for the walkway or wall in memory of your child. These gardens also have an annual memorial service for bereaved parents.

Create a special tradition for your baby's birthday/due date anniversary

Creating a special way for your family to remember this child each year may seem difficult at first, but it can also become a treasured family tradition. It can be helpful for other children in the family to have a way to remember the brother or sister who is not living. We visit Nicholas every year on his birthday and due date, and the boys take great pride in clipping the grass around the stone and scrubbing off any dirt with water and paper towels. The past few times we have done this, they have also gone around and cared for the stones of the other infants buried around Nicholas. Aaron and I also attend the daily mass on Nicholas' birthday each year.

Register your baby's name via the Internet

There are a number of on-line resources where you can register your baby's name. Some of these sites send you support information, and others are just on-line memorials. Some of those resources are listed in the reference section of this book.

Perform a service project for others

There are always organizations looking for help with service projects. Join a team building a house with Habitat for Humanity, a group cleaning up a park, or donate your time in some other way. If you don't want to make a big time commitment, you can take an ornament from one of the holiday Angel Tree/ Toys for Tots type of holiday programs and buy a gift in your child's name for a child of the same age.

Participate in Pregnancy and Infant Loss Awareness Day

In 1988, President Ronald Reagan declared October 15th to be National Pregnancy and Infant Loss Awareness Day. Across the country, memorial services, remembrance walks, and other events are held in memory of all the babies whose lives were too short. My boys and I take flowers to the cemetery on October 15th each year, leaving one on the gravestone of each baby. I place a small sticker on the stem of each flower, noting the date and the reason for the flower.

Awareness Day is also marked by the annual "Wave of Light", where parents light a candle for their child from the hour of 7-8pm. As the candles in one time zone are blown out, the next time zone is lighting theirs, and the light continues, around the world. It is not a public display, but it is comforting to be part of something you know is stretching around the globe, uniting all bereaved parents, for a moment.

If there is nothing available in your area, perhaps you are the person to begin something—not right away, of course, but when you have healed enough to begin looking forward again.

Things to Say and Do

If you have been through the loss of a baby, you have a good idea of what may be helpful to say or offer to someone else who is experiencing the same trauma. For those who are at a loss for what to do for someone experiencing a miscarriage or stillbirth, here are some suggestions:

Acknowledge the loss

Saying "I'm so sorry" may not feel like much, but it brings comfort to the bereaved parents to hear condolences expressed. Offer hugs and gestures of comfort, if appropriate in the relationship.

Offer to be a listening ear

Many women need to talk about their experience. Offer to let the mother talk, knowing you are not there to solve the problem or take away the pain, just to let her express it. Or to just spend time in her presence, if she doesn't want to talk. Sometimes just not being alone can help. And although fathers often don't seem to want to talk about how they are feeling, they should not be ignored. Often asking "How are you doing?" will illicit the response of "I'm fine.", but remembering to offer the ear to the fathers helps them to know they haven't been forgotten in all of this.

Offer to watch other children

If the mother has other children at home, she may appreciate the chance to have some quiet time to herself, to recover physically from the trauma her body has experienced. And the siblings can benefit from some special attention when things in their household have been turned upside down.

Bring a meal

Often newly bereaved people will say there is nothing they need when people ask "What can I do?" And yet, the daily tasks of everyday life can seem overwhelming. Bring dinner, help with housework, run errands—these are things that can be of big help, but will not usually be asked for by the parents. Phrase your offer as a statement: "I'd like to bring you dinner." or "I'm heading to the store—what can I pick up for you?" If the parents say no thanks, offer again in a few days. Sometimes they are so numb, help is hard to accept.

Don't forget about Dad

People check on the mother following a miscarriage, but often people forget about the father. Don't forget, he is hurting, too, and often will feel the need to be strong for everyone else in the family. Ask about Dad when you ask about his wife.

Check back in periodically

People assume after a few weeks that bereaved people are no longer in need of help—the reality is the numbness wears off and the real struggles begin weeks or months following a loss. Check back in with the parents with a phone call, email or card, just to let them know someone is still thinking about them. If you know the baby's due date, send a card or give a call—there may not be many people who remember, and the parents will be very aware of the day as it approaches. Send a card on the baby's birthdate/loss date, for that anniversary will be difficult as well.

A Note to the Medical Field

I was fortunate to have incredible support from my midwife and doctors in dealing with my losses, but many women with whom I have spoken have not been so lucky. We realize that for those who provide care for pregnant women on a daily basis, miscarriage is a very common event. You may see this every day in your practice, and cannot get emotionally involved with every loss. But please remember that for the woman in your office or on the other end of the phone, this loss is heartbreaking. How you handle the few minutes you spend with her can ease or intensify the trauma.

Treat this loss like any other death. What is the first thing a surgeon would say to a family when a patient dies in the operating room? "I'm so sorry." This is no different. Offer your condolences to the parents and take a few extra minutes to offer them what support you can. Don't offer medical statistics on how frequently this occurs, for that just makes the parents feel like what they are experiencing is not important. If there are medical issues that require immediate attention or surgery, obviously, they need to be discussed quickly. If not, offer to answer what questions the parents may have. Keep pamphlets or lists of local support resources in your office, to have something you can give the parents which will help them figure out what to do next. You cannot be the only source of support for each patient coping with this trauma, but you can make them feel, by just a little bit of extra time, that you care about what they are experiencing.

For those who work in emergency departments and are treating women you have never met, try and be as gentle as possible. While emergency rooms are busy, chaotic places and a miscarrying woman who is not critically hemorrhaging is not necessarily high on the priority list of needing attention, remember that for this woman, this is an emergency, this is a trauma. Try to find her space out of the hallway and help her to deal with the bleeding and pain she is experiencing. Remember, she is frightened by what is happening, or she wouldn't be there. Emergency rooms should also have support resources on hand to distribute to parents upon discharge. You cannot make her situation any better, but you can offer kindnesses that ease the trauma, even if only for a short time.

Medical professionals are busy people, often with more patients to see than there are slots in the day. No one expects you to put your day aside and only minister to one patient. But taking a few extra minutes and extending extra kindness to those experiencing a loss of this kind will not put your schedule so far off—and will go a long way towards helping a grieving parent begin to heal.

A Few Final Thoughts

Each person who experiences the death of a baby, through any means, has their own story to tell. Every story is different and each person will walk the journey of grief and healing in their own way, in their own time. Some people will move on quickly, others will take a long time. Remember that your journey is your own—no one else can tell you how long it should take.

As I wrote at the start of this book, there are no words that anyone can say to take this all away from you. There is no magic wand that will put your world back the way it was. Only time can do that, and the world will never be back to exactly the way it was before. It is okay to always carry your baby in your heart and even to shed tears in his or her memory in years to come. As cliché as it sounds, time does heal the wounds. The sun will begin to shine again and life will move forward. Your heart will carry the scars, but it will heal.

I began this book by saying I don't have all the answers. Even those with similar experiences can only offer support, not take your pain away. However, I hope in reading this book you have felt the presence of a friend sitting next to you, offering a hand to hold, a hug when you need it.

May you come to find the place of peace and healing as you continue on life's journey.

Kathleen

Footprints

One night a man had a dream.
He dreamed he was walking along the beach with the Lord
Across the sky flashed scenes from his life.
For each scene, he noticed two sets of footprints in the sand;
One belonging to him, and the other to the Lord.

When the last scene of his life flashed before him,
he looked back at the footprints in the sand.
He noticed that many times along the path of his life,
there was only one set of footprints.
He also noticed that it happened
at the very lowest and saddest times in his life.

This really bothered him and he questioned the Lord about it.
"Lord, you said that once I decided to follow You,
You'd walk with me all the way.
But I have noticed that during the most troublesome
times in my life,
there is only one set of footprints.
I don't understand why when I needed You most,
You would leave me."

The Lord replied,
"My precious, precious child.
I love you and would never leave you.
During your times of trial and suffering
when you see only one set of footprints,
it was then that I carried you.

--Author unknown

Additional Resources

Bereaved Parents of the USA (BPUSA)
http://www.bereavedparentsusa.org

Center for Loss in Multiple Birth (CLIMB), Inc.
http://www.climb-support.org

Mommies Enduring Neonatal Death (MEND)
http://mend.org

Pregnancy Loss and Infant Death Alliance (PLIDA)
http://www.plida.org

> PLIDA provides a network for parents, medical professionals and others interested in increasing awareness and education on the experiences and needs of bereaved parents.

SHARE Pregnancy and Infant Loss Support, Inc.
www.nationalshare.org

> Share offers online and downloadable resources, chat rooms and message boards for parents, a monthly bereavement newsletter, workshop/retreat opportunities for bereaved parents, grandparents and children.

Shrine of the Holy Innocents
128 West 37th Street
New York, NY 10018
212-279-5861
https://shrineofholyinnocents.org/shrine-of-the-unborn

> This Catholic community has a Book of Life in its sanctuary, dedicated to the memory of those who have died unborn. You can register your baby's name on line to be added into the book. Support materials and a certificate of life are also available to parents.

Suggestions for Additional Reading

The following is a list of other books you may find helpful in your journey of healing:

A Silent Love: Personal Stories of Coming to Terms with Miscarriage – Adrienne Ryan

An Empty Cradle, A Full Heart – Christine Lafsler

Coming to Terms with Miscarriage – Jon Cohen

Empty Arms: Coping with Miscarriage and Stillbirth

– Sherokee Ilse

Empty Cradle, Broken Heart – Deborah Davis

Grieving the Child I Never Knew – Kathe Wunnenberg

I'll Hold You in Heaven – Jack Hayford

Letters To Gabriel – Karen Sarturm

The Good Grief Club – Monica Novak

Miscarriage: Women Sharing from the Heart – Marie Allen, PhD and Shelly Marks, MS

Silent Grief – Clara Hinton

When Men Grieve – Elizabeth Levang, Ph.D

Book Suggestions for Children

Am I Still a Sister? – Allie Sims

No New Baby – Marilyn Gryte

No Smile Cookies Today – Kathy Kennedy Tapp

Thumpy's Story – as told to Nancy C. Dodge (also available on video)

Someone Came Before You – Pat Schwiebert

We Were Going to Have a Baby, But We Had an Angel Instead – Pat Schwiebert

Glossary of Medical Terms

Cervix The neck-like opening to the uterus that extends into the vagina. Usually tightly closed, it must open to ten centimeters during labor to allow for the birth of a baby.

D&C The abbreviation for "dilation and curettage." A surgical procedure in which the cervix is forcibly opened to allow the surgeon access to the uterus. Often done when a miscarriage is incomplete, the surgeon either scrapes out the lining of the uterus with a spoon-like device, or uses a vacuum extraction to clean out the contents of the uterus.

Dilate The opening of the cervix during labor. Contractions of the uterus pull the cervix open to ten centimeters, allowing for the passage of the baby from the uterus.

Ectopic pregnancy The developing embryo implants in the wall of the fallopian tube rather than the lining of the uterus. If undetected, the tube will burst between six and eight weeks into the pregnancy, and can be life threatening to the mother. The mother will require emergency surgery to remove the embryo and usually tube itself. Fertility may be reduced but is usually not compromised following the removal of only one tube.

Embryo The term used to describe a developing baby from conception to eight weeks gestation.

Fetus The term used to describe a developing baby from eight weeks gestation to the moment of birth.

Gestation The term used to describe the amount of time a developing baby is carried in the uterus. Gestational age is calculated from the point of conception—thirty-eight weeks is considered to be full term.

Miscarriage   The spontaneous ending of a pregnancy prior to the twentieth week of gestation. Usually causing strong cramps and heavy bleeding as the uterus works to expel an embryo or fetus that has died. Often a D&C is required to completely clean out the contents of the uterus.

Perinatal death   The term for the death of a baby any time from the twentieth week of gestation through the first month of life.

Stillbirth   The term used to describe the death in utero of a baby after twenty weeks gestation.

Sonogram The image produced by ultrasound.

Ultrasound The non-invasive procedure in which sound waves are used to generate an image of a developing baby and uterus on a screen or monitor. Used as a diagnostic tool for detection of developmental problems prior to birth.

You can contact Kathleen at
angelsinmyheart@gmail.com

Made in the USA
Middletown, DE
22 May 2022

66072164R00146